For all my oilfield friends in the Permian Basin

Santa Rita No. 1 in Reagan County, postcard by P. C. McGlasson of San Angelo. Courtesy of DeGolyer Library, Southern Methodist University, Dallas

REINVENTING TEXAS: THE LEGACY OF SANTA RITA Nº 1

BOBBY D. WEAVER

Texas State Historical Association
An Independent Nonprofit Since 1897

AUSTIN, TEXAS

© 2025 Texas State Historical Association.
All rights reserved. Printed in the U.S.A.

LIBRARY OF CONGRESS CATALOGING-IN-PUBLICATION DATA

Name: Weaver, Bobby D., author
Title: Reinventing Texas: The Legacy of Santa Rita No. 1 / Bobby D. Weaver, author
Publisher: Austin: Texas State Historical Association, 2025
Identifiers: LCCN 2024048957 (print) | LCCN 2024048958 (ebook)
   ISBN 9781625110794 (paperback) | ISBN 9781625110824 (hardback)
   ISBN 9781625110800 (ebook)
Subjects: LCSH: Petroleum industry and trade—Texas | University of Texas
   Texas A&M University | Permian Basin (Texas and New Mexico)
Classification: LCC HD9567.T3 W39 2025 (print) | LCC HD9567.T3 (ebook)
   DDC 338.2/728209764—dc23/eng/20250116
LC record available at https://lccn.loc.gov/2024048957
LC ebook record available at https://lccn.loc.gov/2024048958

Cover design by Joel A. Philips,
   from a Tom Lea illustration in Martin W. Schwettmann,
   Santa Rita: The University of Texas Oil Discovery (TSHA, 1943)
Interior design by Neil Ferguson

Texas State Historical Association
P.O. Box 5428
Austin, Texas 78763
(512) 471-2600
www.tshaonline.org

★ CONTENTS

Preface...vii

Introduction.....................................xvii

1. Before Santa Rita No. 1 (1901–1921) 1
2. Drilling Santa Rita No. 1 (1919–1925) 10
3. Expanding the Basin (1923–1930)............... 24
4. A Roof Over Their Heads (1923–1930).......... 38
5. The Work They Did and How it Changed (1923–1930) 56
6. Slowing Down: The Great Depression and World War II Years (1930–1945) 68
7. Expansion and Change (1945–1975)............ 84
8. Deterioration and Rejuvenation (1975–2023)....96
9. The Legacy of Santa Rita No. 1 (2023)......... 106

Index 119

★ PREFACE

THE NINETEENTH CENTURY in Texas ended, and the twentieth began, not with a whimper but with a bang. On September 9, 1900, a storm crashed on the beaches of Galveston with such ferocity that it took the lives of more than 9,000 people, destroyed one third of all the built structures, and secured the dubious ranking of the greatest natural disaster in U.S. history. Texas thus lost the thriving cotton port that played a major role in defining it during the second half of the nineteenth century. In 1901, an oil well known as Spindletop blew in near present-day Beaumont, gushing so freely that it put Texas on the pathway to becoming the world's largest producer of oil. At the same time in Texas, 500 miles to the west, cows were peacefully grazing here and there across 86,000 square miles of semi-arid landscape that would become known as the Permian Basin. They and their owners in this least populated part of Texas knew little or nothing about these events in the eastern part of the state. Certainly, their unanimous conclusion would have been that nothing even closely resembling those two events could ever occur in the isolated desert where they lived.

As Bobby Weaver's book clearly demonstrates, they could never have been further from the truth. Their reality would be redefined in the late spring of 1923 on the eastern edge of the Permian Basin near a place called Big Lake, when crewmen drilled an oil well that bore the name of Santa Rita, patron saint of the impossible or improbable. Weaver is quick to point out the improbability of the success of this endeavor. There had not been a successful well within 100 miles of the location, and there was no surface structure to give any indication that there could be oil below the drill site. As unbelievable as the finding of oil was, the fact that their first effort was drilling a successful water well, a necessity for drilling the oil well and supporting the workers gathered for the event, was astounding. Their successful drilling of a water well close by the prospective oil location was as improbable and rare as finding oil.

The success of Santa Rita No. 1 attracted a flood of individuals who rushed in to participate in the field development, shattering forever the solitude of a vast part of West Texas. The damage inflicted on the landscape was not comparable to the loss of lives and property in Galveston, but it was just as transformative. For those living there who loved the lack of numerous neighbors, this event was met with regret. Weaver points out that the oil workers in the first wave were young, without family, and lived in tents, which proved to be extremely disruptive to existing communities. The rapid influx of people caused serious problems regarding water and sanitation, in addition to a rapid and considerable increase in lawlessness and unruly conduct. The development efforts that Santa Rita No. 1 sparked also encouraged the quick building of roads to move large quantities of supplies across the desert landscape, which does not react well to the impact of civilization. The land does not quickly heal from disruptions to its surface.

As Weaver emphasizes, this desert country had been home to almost no one, in part because it was a nearly waterless environment. The Pecos River bisected the country, but it held mostly alkaline water, while existing springs were far and few between and were only temporary watering holes for those passing through the area. For hundreds of years this had been native Americans. It was a land favored by the Apaches and Comanches, who rarely stayed in one place for very long. The Spanish, who largely avoided the region, called it *El Desplobado*, or "the uninhabited place." Water was certainly the most precious commodity while, for the early inhabitants, oil had little to no use. The country's vast display of solitude and sanctity was best left just as it was, in the opinion of the few calling it home and those just passing through.

But as Weaver points out, centuries of solitude quickly changed after 1923, giving way to the creation of one of the greatest oil regions in the world, with incredible profits for many people and sweeping changes to the arid landscape. Weaver ably captures the wonder of the dramatic and explosive transformation of this unsettled, even romantic, 86,000 square miles of near desert over a period of 100 years into an oil and gas Mecca like almost none elsewhere in the world today. While the environment and water shortages remain important concerns, the oil fields of the Permian Basin, beginning with Santa Rita No. 1, continue to define a substantial sector of the modern Texas economy.

Weaver speaks to his readers as an insightful reporter, using language and phrases foreign to the narrative style of most academics but familiar to those individuals who devoted their lives and spent their fortunes to developing the Permian Basin into one of the largest oil and gas producing areas in Texas, the United States, and even the world. Because of the now famous Santa Rita No. 1 well, which initially produced only 200 barrels a day, the region sponsored some 7,000 producing fields, and 100 years later 2 billion barrels of oil a year. Weaver, with folksy vernacular and brilliant insight, captures the individual struggles of bringing oil development to the Permian Basin against all odds—the forces of nature and the lack of water, roads, rails, and other infrastructure. By today's standards, early drilling was slow and labor-intensive, but those engaged in it were up to the task. Weaver tells the stories of boomtowns, oil camps, horse-drawn wagons rolling over sand hills nearly impossible to cross in the cars and trucks of the day, and many more. He also brings to life the characters who made fortunes in this effort and those who lost everything, men like Frank T. Pickrell, who raised the money for Santa Rita No. 1, and Carl G. Cromwell who drilled the famous well. Most importantly, he documents the incredible economic impact of the Permian Basin's oil and gas resources on the region, the state of Texas, and Texas's institutions for higher education. He fills his pages with literary images of a place that had no cities and a population that numbered no more than a few thousand people, but quickly became a region with many smaller communities, four cities of major economic significance—Midland, Odessa, San Angelo, and Abilene—and a population of over 1.4 million people, many of whom work today in the industry made possible by that small well, Santa Rita No. 1, named for the patron saint of the impossible.

It has been said that this part of West Texas is a country that promises little and gives much. This is certainly demonstrated vividly in the pages of this book. It all began with that first wave of individuals descending on this barren landscape with the force of a hurricane, who brought a new culture and prosperity that came from that single resource in which they were in pursuit - black gold. Unlike almost all other economic endeavors, it came not from the surface of the land, but beneath the earth.

To this desert landscape came individuals with high ambitions to transform what was there, to redefine the land with all of its mystery, wonder, and solitude. But ultimately the place changed them as much as they changed it, just as a gift of over 1,000,000 acres of seemingly worthless land to endow a state university of the first class became incredibly valuable because of Santa Rita No. 1. It changed dramatically the funding available to Texas educational institutions. Some say that as education goes at the University of Texas and Texas A&M University, so goes education elsewhere in Texas. Texas higher education has succeeded thanks to Santa Rita No. 1. More than $1 trillion in oil revenue has been produced in the Permian Basin over its 100-year history, and the Permanent University Fund has become the largest educational endowment in the United States. The story of that event and the impact of what the oil industry has in the Permian Basin and throughout Texas has been ignored too long by the academic community. Weaver's book provides the grist from which future historians can grind out wonderful stories about the industry, the numerous characters it sponsored, and the incredible prosperity they have provided our state and nation.

Thankfully, this rousingly good book about one of the most important economic events in U.S. history, the success of Santa Rita No. 1 and the eventual development of over 7,000 oil and gas fields in the Permian Basin, has finally been published. It is an accomplishment that matches in economic importance the building of such better-known icons as the transcontinental railroad, Erie Canal, Brooklyn Bridge, and intercoastal waterway, and it also demonstrates the ingenuity and creativity of American business when it is unleashed by our free enterprise system.

The Permian Basin is a showcase for the enormous technological development that has distinguished the oil industry for over a century. It has advanced from painfully slow cable tool drilling, under the watchful eye of the drill foreman like in the days of drilling Santa Rita No. 1, to such incredible advances as seismic interpretation of oil formations far below the earth's surface, horizontal drilling, positive displacement drilling motors that bore straight laterals in long-reach horizontal wells, and highly sophisticated well fracking. Many of these functions are now directed by computers, not humans. All these advances have allowed the oil and gas industry to deliver to people in the United States the lowest fuel costs of any nation in the world, facilitating the development of the greatest economic power ever.

This is a story worth telling, and the credit for initiating this publication goes to William R. "Billy" Murphy Jr., CEO of University Lands for the University of Texas System. His first interest was in reprinting the book *Santa Rita*, originally published in 1943 by a team of Texans. Walter Prescott Webb, an award-winning Texas historian and the director of the Texas State Historical Association, had the idea for the book. He directed his graduate student, Martin W. Schwettmann, in writing a master's thesis on Santa Rita No. 1, which became the book. Sadly, this proved to be Schwettman's only book. Carl Hertzog, the finest book designer in Texas, laid his hand on all the cosmetic features of the publication; and the illustrations were contributed by Tom Lea, who is certainly one of the best artists to call Texas home. If all these contributions were not enough, overseeing the effort was Stanley Marcus, the owner of Neiman Marcus. Stanley, famous for his love of beautiful books, was also the founder of the Book Club of Texas. These men published a beautiful, historically informative, and exceedingly scarce literary jewel in a limited edition of only 440 copies. Then Murphy requested a book detailing the history of the development of oil in the Permian Basin and the incredible impact it had on both the University Fund and the state of Texas, to commemorate the centennial of the discovery of Santa Rita No. 1 on the University Lands. We at the TSHA could not have been more pleased by this two-part request for a reprint of a classic and a new book.

There has been a paucity of historical research and publications by the academic community on clearly one of the most compelling and important industries in the entire state of Texas, the oil and gas industry. It has attracted all the characters, drama, and lively stories that are the necessary embellishments for interesting and inspiring history. It is our hope that this book by Weaver will be the spark for many histories of the oil industry and the personalities that built it. Weaver's book profiles many potential subjects deserving further historical investigation, such as the two key individuals who ignited the Permian Basin oil empire, Pickrell, the promoter of the deal, and Cromwell, the driller who found his way from Pennsylvania to Texas. Men such as these are nearly omnipresent personalities at almost every historically large oil discovery in Texas. The same could be said for Haymon Krupp, founder of Texon Oil and Land Company. He was a partner in drilling Santa Rita No. 1, the largest Jewish clothing dealer in El Paso, and a renowned local philanthropist.

Weaver also provides important insights into the problem of providing proper housing for the workforce, not tents as was the common solution for earlier arrivals, but commodious living spaces. There was one effort to build a town just for oil field employees, named Texon for the company by the same name, but the most unique concept for housing were the camps. The camps actually first appeared on the Texas Gulf Coast and were perfected by the time they arrived in the Permian Basin. They provided homes for oil company employees and, while they stopped far short of being incorporated cities, offered many amenities such as swimming pools and tennis courts. They became communities that hosted regular holiday gatherings and other events. They were located near towns in order to provide bus service to nearby schools, which offered excellent educational opportunities since they were supported by significant tax revenues from the producing oil fields. All the major oil companies had these unique living sites, where they not only built the homes but let the families live there for free.

Camps not only provided shelter but created a sense of community. All employees shared a common purpose, to oversee the efficient and profitable production of oil and gas for the company for which they all worked. This included transporting oil and gas to markets east and west. Unlike the first wave of workers, who were mostly young men appropriately known as roughnecks and roustabouts who came for adventure and good pay, those that came to the camps were families. The camps became homogeneous communities brought together by the necessity of attracting capable employees and sustained by the satisfaction of those who chose to stay. This is a unique chapter in the oil and gas industry, and there are many human stories embedded in the fifty-year history of camps that are waiting to be evaluated and told by future historians. These are only a few modest suggestions that emerge from the pages of Weaver's book. Weaver could very well have said this, quoting Webb, "It seems to me that oil is the current topic about which much history of Texas will crystallize during the next century. All the literature having to do with the beginning of this industry is sure to be sought after by collectors and historians, some of them are already alive to the future importance of this category of Texana." To this, we can add that certainly nothing identifies modern Texans, by choice or by chance, better than oil men and oil women.

J. P. Bryan, Executive Director
Texas State Historical Association

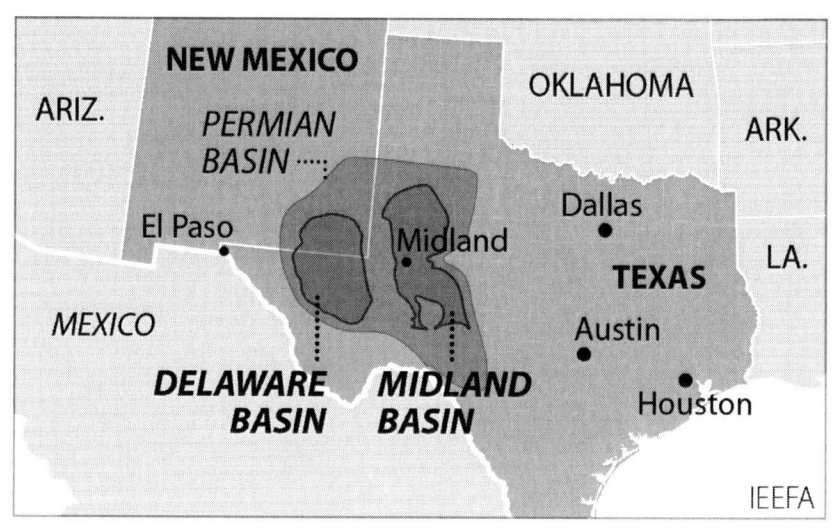

Courtesy of IEEFA
[https://ieefa.org/articles/ieefa-us-pioneer-other-independents-top-supermajor-production-permian-basin]

★ INTRODUCTION

SOMEWHERE, OUT BEYOND the hundredth meridian, there lies a magical land. Most see it as just another place, but to me it is more of a spiritual thing, where the impossible can and does happen. It is a land that warms the heart with sunsets that glow bright red and orange and eventually fade into velvety purple just at nightfall. Within that magical world, unimaginably beautiful landscapes exist like mirages shimmering in the distance. It is peopled by a race of giants whose remarkable feats have left their mark upon the land. The imagination of people the world over has been captivated by it. Artists with brush and canvas, writers with pen and ink, and denizens of Tinseltown with their silver screens have all tried their hand at capturing the totality of that magical realm. But in the end, they have managed to give us only a glimpse of its grandeur.

Those with little romance in their souls might reject my vision of this land. For them it is simply that geographic region called the American West. This begins roughly at the hundredth meridian, where the less-than-twenty-inch annual rainfall line lies, and it stretches westward to the Pacific Ocean. It is the largest geographic region in the United States. It contains all the deserts in the country and most of the mountain ranges, at least the highest ones. In general, it is mostly an arid land that early explorers dubbed "the Great American Desert." Its reputation intimidated timid souls dwelling in the well-watered lands to the East, resulting in that magical land being the last major geographic region in the nation to be settled.

Tucked away in one of the isolated corners of that magical land lies a special place. Its surface is covered with a scraggly growth of thorny vegetation. It has always had few inhabitants and even fewer notable geographic features. It is one of those places where you can stand and seemingly see forever. For many, that empty vastness appears frightening and makes them feel small and insignificant, but for others it offers a mind-expanding experience with unlimited opportunity. That place would become known as the Permian Basin.

At the beginning of the 1920s, the Permian Basin was one of those largely unknown and ignored places in far West Texas. Then a little oil well was drilled there, producing only about 200 barrels per day, a small, unimpressive accomplishment. But the little well had been blessed in the name of Santa Rita, the patron saint of impossible causes. It was called Santa Rita No. 1, and it ignited a spark that grew into an economic conflagration that became the nation's most productive oil producing region and transformed a tiny rural ranching population into an urban, petroleum-oriented culture. It also produced one of the largest endowments supporting higher education in Texas and the United States.

In 2023, one hundred years after that little well began producing, its legacy, born in that forgotten corner of the magical land out beyond the hundredth meridian, is alive and well. The fire it ignited still burns brightly, not only in the Permian Basin, where a dynamic oilfield culture produces a significant part of the nation's energy, but in its support of higher education within the state of Texas. To the best of my knowledge there is no patron saint of the oil patch, but if there was, Santa Rita would get my vote.

Big Lake, in Reagan County, in the early twentieth century.
Courtesy of Portal to Texas History

1 BEFORE SANTA RITA NO. 1 (1901–1921)

THE TWO MOST FAMOUS OIL WELLS in Texas are Lucas No. 1 (Spindletop) and Santa Rita No. 1. Spindletop set the stage for petroleum to replace cotton and cattle as the economic mainstay of the state, and Santa Rita No. 1 opened the Permian Basin to become the largest oil and gas producing area in the United States as well as transforming higher education in Texas.

Spindletop came in on January 10, 1901, and blew wild for nine days at an estimated rate of 100,000 barrels per day before it was finally capped. That unprecedented phenomenon, in a day when few wells produced more than a hundred barrels per day, focused worldwide attention on what seemed to be an endless supply of future oil in Texas.

Slightly more than two decades later, on May 28, 1923, Santa Rita No. 1 came in much less spectacularly at less than 200 barrels per day. But that event was destined to spark a legacy that has left an indelible mark on the state of Texas. First, it established the Permian Basin as the largest oil-producing region in the nation, and second, it was the first oil well to drill on state land reserved for support of higher education in Texas, which ultimately helped fund one of the largest educational endowments in the nation.

Following the Spindletop discovery, petroleum exploration spread out across the state with unbridled success. Within twenty years, new discoveries created oil fields all along the Gulf Coast and north and west, making Texas the top oil-producing state in the country. Places like Sour Lake, Batson, Petrolia, Burkburnett, Ranger, Eastland, Desdemona, and scores of other towns experienced massive oil booms and became household names.

When that first discovery happened, there were only a handful of people in Texas who knew anything about the oil business. Consequently, in those very early days experienced oil people from Pennsylvania and West Virginia flocked to the state to work. That small core of oilfield workers was totally inadequate to get the job done, so local people from the Lone Star State's mostly rural population were recruited to fill the need. The multitude of relatively unskilled but well-paid occupations available in the oilfields proved to be an irresistible draw to thousands of young men who left the farm to work in the "oil patch." In the jargon of the industry, the "oil patch" replaced the cotton patch as a workplace, while the newcomers were called "boll weevils" in reference to their agricultural backgrounds.

That process settled into a pattern of hiring local labor when an oil boom developed. When that boom passed, some of them moved elsewhere to the next boom, some stayed to work in the local oilfield, and some returned to their former jobs. By 1920, when the expansion of oil and gas activity in Texas bumped up against the eastern edge of the Permian Basin, a substantial cadre of native Texans were working in oilfields scattered in many areas of the state.

The Permian Basin comprises a huge expanse of territory. It extends approximately 300 miles from near Lubbock on the north to Pecos County on the south, and 250 miles from near Colorado City on the east to the Pecos River Valley and southeastern New Mexico on the west. It includes all or parts of more than 50 counties and contains more than 86,000 square miles of land. It is a semi-arid to arid region that was then, and still is today, one of the least populated sections of the state.

In 1920, the Permian Basin did not have a single mile of paved roadway, leaving local travel to primitive, sandy ranch roads that were little more than cattle trails. The region was served on its northerly side by the Texas and Pacific Railway (T&P), which ran west from Fort Worth to El Paso via Abilene, Midland, Odessa, and Pecos. Its southern section was served by the Kansas City, Mexico, and Orient Railway (popularly known as the Orient), which rolled west from San Angelo to Presidio via Big Lake, Rankin, Fort Stockton, and Alpine.

Geologically, the Permian Basin is a huge, subsurface basin with thick sedimentary formations that were created during the Permian geological period, from which it derives its name. Additionally, there are numerous other major geological features within its confines. Among those are the Midland Basin, the Delaware Basin, the Central Basin Platform, and several others, all of which produce oil and gas. Consequently, the Permian Basin became home to more than 7,000 separate oilfields discovered between 1920 and the present. Of course, in 1920 all that data was unknown, although a few geologists had speculated that oil and gas resources might exist in the region.

Most legendary activities present a variety of misconceptions, which tend to crop up concerning firsts. One of those is that Santa Rita No. 1, completed in 1923, was the first producing oil well drilled in the Permian Basin, which confuses the issue because firsts are not always the most important. The first producing oil well drilled in the Permian Basin was the T&P Abrams No. 1, completed in June 1920 on the Basin's far eastern side, a couple of miles northwest of Westbrook in Mitchell County.

The Underwriters Producing & Refining Company had begun leasing activities in the area late in 1919, hired a well-known wildcat driller named Steven S. Owen, and spudded in on the Abrams No. 1

early in 1920. By February 8, at a depth of 450 feet, the well had a slight showing of oil and gas, and drilling ended in late June 1920 at a depth of 2,987 feet. Amidst the usual ballyhoo surrounding the initial production, it was scheduled to be shot with nitroglycerin on July 16, 1920. The widely advertised event was attended by a large crowd that included more than 2,000 excited spectators, who got their money's worth. The shot blew mud, water, and, more importantly, oil high over the derrick, to the delight of the host of visiting oil men, investors, and ordinary citizens.

At the time, Abrams No. 1 was touted as being a 2,000-barrel-per-day producer, although that number was quickly reduced downward to a permanent rate of 100. Nevertheless, excitement created by the discovery stirred up interest in a hitherto disregarded region of the state, far removed from proven production. Over the course of several years, the area of the Abrams discovery, known as the Westbrook Field, expanded in size to about six miles long by two miles wide. Over the next ten decades the field produced more than 100 million barrels of oil and prompted the development of 21 smaller fields in Mitchell County. But it never expanded to any regional significance and was largely ignored in the larger scheme of things.

By 1922 the production from Abrams No. 1 prompted H. L. Lockhart to build the first commercial pipeline in the Permian Basin. Two years afterward, as increased production warranted, the Col-Tex Refinery was built on a 175-acre site just west of Colorado City. With the distinction of being the first oil refinery in the Permian Basin, that plant remained in operation until 1969 and was dismantled in the early 1970s.

Meanwhile, excitement created by Abrams No. 1 caused oil fever to spread westward. In 1921, the second commercial discovery in the Permian Basin was made on its western edge in Loving County. That area was the most sparsely populated area in the state and in 1920 boasted only 82 citizens. The next year, J. J. Wheat and Baden Ramsey organized the Toyah-Bell Oil Company and leased acreage on the Russell Ranch about one mile east of the present-day town of Mentone. At that time, Loving was not an organized county after an attempt at organization had been abandoned due to insufficient population as early as the 1890s. It was not until 1931 that Loving County officially organized, and it has always struggled to maintain a population hovering around 100 people.

In the summer of 1921, the Toyah-Bell Oil Company spudded in Russell No. 1, and by December the completed well was flowing enough oil to be considered a commercial success. At that point the company changed its name to the Ramsey Oil Company, signed a contract to deliver oil to the Rio Grande Oil and Refining Company in El Paso at a price of $3 dollars per barrel, and built a four-inch pipeline to the Pecos River Railroad siding of Arno a few miles away. Over time, the Ramsey Oil Company maintained enough production from the Wheat Field, as the discovery became known, to continue operating for the next one hundred years.

The two discoveries in 1920 and 1921, representing the Permian Basin's first commercial oil production, first pipeline, and first refinery, were more than two hundred miles apart. Although they were a portent of things to come, at the time no connection was made between the two events. How that space became filled with a host of producing oil fields that changed the face of the land, helped create an oilfield culture, produced massive support for higher education in Texas, and provided unbelievable wealth for the people of the state—all begun by the drilling of Santa Rita No. 1—is a remarkable story.

For that to come to pass there were several difficulties to overcome. First and foremost was the nature of the land itself. The Permian Basin is a hard land where water is rare and precious and everything that grows seems to have thorns of one kind or another.

That landscape presented early-day oilmen with numerous difficulties unique to the region. To begin, the only roads were little more than sandy tracks leading to lonely ranch houses miles away from the nearest neighbors. Unlike lands farther east, where travel became difficult only when it rained, the terrain presented a constant problem because the deep loose sand was always there, causing the underpowered, chain-driven trucks of the day to be totally unusable. Freight was delivered to railroad depots and then transported to well sites and other locations by horse- and mule-powered wagons, while motorized vehicles were used primarily for short hauls from railway sidings to warehouses. Wagon and team operations did the bulk of the hauling, quartering their animals at a myriad of locations, usually in groups of about one hundred. Although skilled teamsters handling multiple hitches of animals presented a colorful spectacle, maintaining large numbers of livestock presented major difficulties.

All the oil drilling rigs in the 1920s were constructed of wood, and the cable-tool drilling operations were powered by steam. Water and fuel for the boilers were always in short supply in that arid environment. Many drilling rigs ran twenty-four hours, seven days per week, and at night had to be lighted by small, open-flamed lanterns called "yellow dogs" that looked for all the world like Aladdin's lamps. It takes very little imagination to visualize the danger of working on a gassy drilling rig with several open-flamed lighting devices cluttering up the space. Electric generators were just coming into vogue in those early days of activity in the Permian Basin.

Beyond the environmental concerns, the most significant problem facing the operation was how to service the overwhelming volume of manpower necessary to drill and supply an oilfield in such an arid and sparely settled region. The number of crewmen needed to drill hundreds of oil wells paled in comparison to the amount required to support that activity. First on the scene were huge numbers of teamsters to transport freight, grade roads, build drilling locations, and do all the preparatory tasks necessary to start drilling operations. Then came the rig builders, whose five- to eight-man crews built every one of the wooden drilling rigs on every location and returned either to tear down the derricks or skid them to new locations when the wells were completed. Once the drilling crews began their work, it took a veritable army of oilfield supply people scurrying about, providing "rope, dope, and soap." Once again, the freighters came into play, transporting all those supplies.

By the time the wells were completed, the tank builders had to construct thousands of field storage tanks as well as huge 55,000- and 80,000-barrel tanks at tank farms, where oil was stored until it could be put on a pipeline. Then the pipeliners arrived, like swarms of locusts, in crews of one hundred men to lay lines out of the area to refineries or to the various railheads where oil was shipped in railway tank cars. There were always roustabouts, the entry-level people of the oil patch who did the common labor necessary to support the more skilled activity. Roustabouts made up the largest number of workers. Altogether, it took a myriad of jobs to create an oilfield and keep it operating in an efficient manner.

The thousands of workers in the first human wave that descended upon any developing area were generally considered "boomers," or contract laborers of a more or less temporary nature. The second wave came shortly afterward, bringing in permanent oil company employees to operate the field as it became drilled, adding to the overcrowding. Distances were vast, and there were hardly any towns. How to feed, shelter, clothe, and entertain a huge influx of people in a region practically devoid of population was perhaps the greatest challenge. In the very earliest days, the work crews lived in tents or small, skid-mounted shacks. A few towns popped up in the fields, but they were for the most part temporary tent-and-shack communities consistent with the

Oil rig workers in Crane County during the 1920s.
Courtesy of Portal to Texas History

traditional oil boom towns of the past.

The almost total lack of proper housing caused the oil companies to develop a "camp" system for housing their permanent employees, those who constituted the second wave of workers to any boom. Camps ranged in size from a few well-built houses to more than a hundred homes within a community that had all the amenities of many towns of the time. The camp system became one of the region's prime characteristics that continued in operation until the 1960s, when improved transportation allowed workers to live farther from their work sites.

So it was that two largely forgotten oil discoveries on opposite sides of the Permian Basin set the stage for the future development of the phenomenon that would become the state's most prolific oil and gas region. During the next one hundred years, the Permian Basin would become the location of a tremendous economic resource despite great geographic and technological challenges. In 1920, it was only awaiting a spark to set it off.

Santa Rita No. 1 on June 10, 1923.
Courtesy of Portal to Texas History

2 DRILLING SANTA RITA NO. 1 (1919–1925)

THE SPARK THAT SET OFF the chain of events that opened up the Permian Basin to major oil and gas production, and transformed funding for higher education in Texas, was the drilling of Santa Rita No. 1. Like any successful well-drilling operation, it can be divided into three distinct segments: obtaining the lease, drilling a producing well, and expanding that initial success. In the case of Santa Rita No. 1, each of those steps was fraught with varying degrees of difficulty.

Obtaining the lease did not follow the usual practice of dealing with a variety of private landholders. Instead, it was developed by leasing a huge block of public lands belonging to the State of Texas. When the Republic of Texas joined the United States in 1845, it was allowed to retain all its public lands. Over time, the state utilized those lands for various matters of public good. One of those dealt with supporting education within the state.

In 1876 the new Texas Constitution called for the creation of the University of Texas (UT) and appropriated one million acres of West Texas land to support this purpose. Using this grant as its catalyst, the Constitution also established the Permanent University Fund (PUF), and these one million acres became forever known as "the constitutional million." Texas legislators added an additional one million acres to the University Lands in 1883 – the same year that UT officially opened with a single building in Austin. UT quietly grew during its first forty years, and then things accelerated when Santa Rita No. 1 struck oil in 1923.

As oil flowed from Santa Rita No. 1, revenue fed into the PUF and sparked development for UT in the 1920s and 1930s, when 23 buildings went up to create the core of the modern Austin campus, including the iconic UT "Tower." In 1931, the Texas Legislature added Texas A&M University (TAMU) as a PUF beneficiary and authorized a division in net income from PUF investments that still exists today – with UT receiving two-thirds of the funds and Texas A&M receiving one-third. As of August 31, 2023, the PUF was valued at $33.01 billion and supported 28 UT and TAMU institutions and agencies that collectively enrolled more than 500,000 students. Funding from the PUF has been used to build classrooms, labs, hospitals and clinics that are needed to educate the state's future workforce, conduct research, and provide healthcare to millions of patients.

The leasing of some of the University Lands, which resulted in the drilling of Santa Rita No. 1, began with the efforts of Rupert P. Ricker, a native of Reagan County, who in 1915 earned a law degree from UT before entering the Army in World War I. Upon being discharged from the service, he returned to Big Lake to find the area suffering from an extended drought. Business opportunities were few and far between. Upon investigation, Ricker discovered that in 1916 Dr. Johan A. Udden, director of the Bureau of Economic Geology at UT, had submitted a report to the Board of Regents concerning the possibility of oil in and around Reagan County.

Recognizing a golden business opportunity, Ricker persuaded a group of local businessmen to band together and lease some of the University property for the purpose of drilling oil wells. In February of 1919 they filed an application for leasing parcels of the University Lands in Reagan, Irion, Upton, and Crockett counties, which amounted to 674 sections or 431,360 acres (almost two-thirds of the 1,091 sections, or 698,390 acres, of the University land in these counties). Then they filed for drilling permits for 171 oil and gas wells. The idea was to sell the drilling permits to pay for the annual lease costs, which at ten cents per acre came to $43,136. They had thirty days in which to tender payment on the leases.

It would be a great idea if it worked. Unfortunately, Ricker was initially unable to find any buyers for the project. With only a few days left to complete the deal, he was in Fort Worth looking for investors when he had a chance encounter with an old Army buddy named Frank T. Pickrell, of El Paso. As it happened, Pickrell was in town with a business associate named Haymon Krupp for the purpose of acquiring large blocks of oil leases on speculation. Pickrell and Krupp agreed to buy the rights to the leases and drilling permits of the Big Lake group at the bargain price of $2,500, of which only $500 accrued to Ricker, which probably did not even pay his expenses. The new owners paid the one-year lease on March 27, 1919, with the intent of reselling at a profit strictly as a real estate transaction. Accordingly, Krupp went to New York to arrange for the sale, but he had absolutely no success.

Eager to recoup their investment, the partners decided to turn the real estate venture into an oil business, about which they knew very little. So, in April 1919 they formed the Texon Oil and Land Company, capitalized at 2,000,000 shares with a par value of one dollar per share. They assigned 900,000 stock shares to the company to cover operational expenses and kept the remaining 1,100,000 shares for themselves. Krupp was named president, and Pickrell became vice president and general manager. The lease size belonging to the company was soon downsized to 200,000 acres from the original 431,360 in order to reduce the annual leasing fee. At that point, Krupp returned to El Paso to care for his considerable personal business operations, and Pickrell assumed the responsibility of managing the new company. His first task was to organize a sales force to sell stock in order to finance the drilling of oil wells. That did not go well.

Selling stock in a wildcat Texas oil company with no production proved difficult. As a result, Pickrell and Krupp went to Burkburnett, in Wichita County, Texas, where Krupp personally paid $25,000 for a lease with three producing wells in the name of the company to "sweeten the pot." Stock sales still remained slow, and time was running out on retaining the drilling permits unless they could show they were actually drilling a well. Pickrell then devised another fund-raising device called "Certificates of Interest." The idea was to divide the lease into blocks of sixteen sections (10,240 acres) and sell certificates of interest representing a tiny, five-acre equity in each particular block. He managed to sell 685 certificates in Block No. 1 for $200 per certificate.

The difficulty of raising the funds necessary to drill the discovery well for the Texon Oil and Land Company, destined to be called Santa Rita No. 1, provides a classic example of a "poor boy" operation. In the course of overseeing the sale of his certificates of interest in New York, Pickrell received notice early in January 1921 that unless he started drilling operations by midnight on January 8, his drilling permits would lapse. Hurrying back to West Texas, he arrived in San Angelo on January 5 and managed to locate a ramshackle portable drilling rig forty miles north of town. He bought the rig and had it hauled to San Angelo for loading on an Orient Railway car for transport ninety miles west to the siding at Best, located about twelve miles west of Big Lake. The train was scheduled to leave at 6 a.m. on January 8, but Pickrell persuaded officials to delay their departure until noon so that he could load the rig.

The train arrived at Best around 5 p.m., and the rig was unloaded and transported about four miles to the proposed drilling site. Drilling began shortly after sundown on what Pickrell called "oil well #1 in block #1," but which was actually the water well necessary to service the operation. A couple of weeks later, Pickrell had the location surveyed for registration with the Texas Railroad Commission, and geologist Hugh H. Tucker drove the stake for the drilling of Santa Rita No. 1 at a point 174 feet north of the railroad and about 40 feet from the water well.

To provide legal proof that drilling had begun at the well site before the midnight deadline on January 8, it was necessary to have a signed and notarized affidavit by two disinterested parties to the effect that they had witnessed the event. Sometime after dark on the day drilling began on the water well, Pickrell spied the headlights of a car in the distance, He flagged it down and persuaded the two men in the vehicle to stop and observe the drilling machine at work. He then rode with them to San Angelo, where they agreed to sign the document for the reward of a box of cigars each. Both witnesses were suspicious of the legality of their involvement, and one of them refused to sign, but evidently the document with only one signature served its purpose.

Meanwhile, the driller pitched a tent and camped while drilling the water well. He struck water at 150 feet early in June 1921, but due to the prolonged drought, it quickly dried up. The well had to be deepened to 425 feet, and there by mid-August a more dependable supply was found. Meanwhile, with the drilling permit secured, the water well approaching completion, and the oil well location marked, Pickrell located a rig builder in Big Spring, seventy miles away, to build the rig and living quarters on the site for $1,000. Pickrell provided all materials. The rig builder, R.S. McDonald, arrived on location with his crew and construction equipment after an arduous cross-country trip. Between the first of July and the end of the month, their work was completed. The rig was a standard Mid-continent-style cable tool drilling rig with a 20-foot by 8-foot cellar, a 20-foot-square drilling floor, and a 72-foot-high wooden derrick. For living quarters, they also built two shotgun-style houses, commonly called "boxcar houses" due to their size and shape.

While the rig was being built, Pickrell found an experienced driller and persuaded him to drill in the wilds of West Texas a long way from anywhere by offering the unusually high wage of $15 per day plus stock in the Texon Oil and Land Company. That man was 32-year-old Carl G. Cromwell, a cable tool driller originally from Pennsylvania, who had been following oil booms since his teenage years. Cromwell, who was working in Cisco, Texas, at the time, located all the drilling tools, boiler, steam engine, band wheel, bull wheels, cabling, and all the other equipment necessary to complete the rig. All that equipment was delivered to the site and scattered helter skelter around the Best railroad siding sometime around the middle of July 1921. With the help of local ranchers acting as teamsters, Cromwell was able to transport the equipment to the drill site and assemble an operating drilling rig in about a month's time. By then he was living in one of the boxcar houses with his wife Luella and their young daughter Carlene, while the other boxcar was occupied by a tool dresser named Crawford K. Stillwagon. The well was spudded in on August 17, 1921, with orders to drill to a maximum of 4,000 feet or until he found oil and gas.

Just prior to beginning the drilling operation Pickrell performed one of the most unusual actions recorded in oilfield history when he climbed the derrick and christened the well Santa Rita No. 1. He explained it in a 1969 interview:

> The name Santa Rita originated in New York. Some of the stock salesmen had encouraged a group of Catholic women to invest in the Group 1 certificates. These women became a little worried about the wisdom of their investment and consulted with

Carl G. Cromwell with his wife, Luella, and daughter, Carlene, at Santa Rita No. 1.
Courtesy of Judy Boreham Dawson

their priest. He apparently was also somewhat skeptical and suggested that the women invoke the help of Santa Rita, who was the patron saint of the impossible. As I was leaving New York on one of my subsequent trips to the field, two of these women handed me a sealed envelope and told me that the envelope contained a red rose that had been blessed by the priest in the name of the saint. The women asked me to take the rose back to Texas with me—to climb to the top of the derrick and scatter the rose petals, which by then were dry, over the rig and to say 'I hereby christen thee Santa Rita.' I faithfully followed these instructions.

This ceremony has become part of the treasured lore of the PUF, as it marked a key turning point in the history of financing higher education in Texas.

The drilling that began on that day became a long and tedious process interrupted by a series of problems of one kind or another. Perhaps the greatest of those was keeping laborers, whether they were qualified or not, willing to work in such an isolated location. The original tool dresser only lasted a short while, and Cromwell was unable to find another experienced man. Consequently, he was forced to depend upon the sporadic help of itinerant cowboys or anybody else he could cajole into working. Although he continued drilling pretty much by himself, it was impossible to keep the rig operating on a regular schedule.

Finally, in January 1922 help arrived in the form of twenty-four-year-old Dee Locklin. He had been working as a tool dresser in the recently discovered Wheat Field in Loving County and was on his way to his home near Big Lake. As he was making his way across country, he spied the lone derrick at Best and could hardly believe his eyes. He stopped to investigate what was going on in the middle of nowhere, and Cromwell hired him on the spot. Locklin brought his young wife, Nora, out to live in the spare shotgun house, and there they stayed until the well came in about seventeen months later.

The well drilling proceeded at a snail's pace. With the nearest supply houses located in Fort Worth, drillers often had to stop work for a week or more while awaiting delivery of replacement parts. Their work was hindered by almost every problem imaginable, ranging from a variety of fishing jobs to a lack of proper tools. The truth of the matter is that they were never able to keep the rig running on a twenty-four-hour basis and averaged less than five feet per day over the course of the job. Plus, as Locklin remembered in a 1969 interview, "We often went as much as three or four months at a time without a paycheck."

Finally, on Sunday afternoon, May 27, 1923, at a depth of 3,050 feet, the two-man crew got a showing of oil while bailing the well. When they ran the bailer back into the hole, it came up filled with oil. They dropped the bailer back in the hole, nailed down a cover on the opening in the drilling floor, and shut the operation down for the day after nailing boards between the drilling legs to prevent any visitors from seeing what was happening. Around seven o'clock the next morning, as the driller and his "toolie" were having breakfast in their respective houses, they heard a roaring sound. Upon rushing outside, they witnessed oil pulsing from the well head. It ebbed and flowed several times until it eventually blew over the top of the derrick. Then after about thirty minutes it dropped to just a trickle. And then it started the routine all over again.

As Locklin explained in a 1970 interview, the drilling crew reacted in the true entrepreneurial spirit of the oilfield of the day:

> We...were not going to work the next day, we were going to buy some leases around the country, which we did. We did that because we knew we had oil, we didn't know how much, but we

> actually knew that much before the well began to blow. Then the well blew in. There wasn't much we could do about it. We just had to go on. We got twenty or thirty sections leased, I can't remember for sure. We got it all in one day. It was quite a bit of country to cover, but we made all the ranches and made the deal right there. Then we went over to the courthouse which was at Stiles at that time and had the papers drawn up.

By the time that the oil men returned that evening to their drill site, a sizable crowd had gathered. Luella Cromwell posted guards to keep them away from the well. It continued to blow in that same pattern once or twice daily, at an estimated flow between thirty and a hundred barrels a day. In late June the casing arrived, and the well could be shut in. In the interim, Carl Cromwell hired local ranchers to dig earthen tanks to hold the oil. Eventually, two 200-barrel tanks were built to hold the overflow. When the well was finally brought under control and put on the pump, it produced two hundred barrels per day, which was shipped by rail to the Rio Grande Oil and Refining Company refinery in El Paso.

The discovery did not make an immediate big splash. The general feeling was expressed by a story that appeared in the *San Angelo Daily Standard* on May 29, 1923:

> Owing to frequent reports of good oil showings in West Texas, which never have panned out profitably, oil men and the public in general have been slow to credit reports of a promising discovery well west of Big Lake, and we are inclined to await further developments before rushing into the prospective new field, but operators and others who have visited the well are confident that at last a real oil showing that will prove to be more than a flash in the pan has been obtained.

Pickrell realized that he had neither the resources nor the expertise to develop the infrastructure necessary to expand drilling and operate the leases under Texon's control. He spent the summer of 1923 looking for a company to buy part of the field without success. Finally, on October 5, he struck a deal with legendary independent Pennsylvania oilman Michael L. Benedum to transfer blocks 1, 2, and 9 to Benedum's newly formed Big Lake Oil Company for $200,000 and one-fourth interest in the new company. Over the next few months several wells, some producing in the 1,000-barrel-per-day range, established the Big Lake Field as an area of approximately four and one-half square miles that was producing at a depth of 3,000 to 3,500 feet. Five years later, its production significantly increased with another pay zone in the 8,000-foot range. The expansion of the Big Lake Field proved that there were significant oil reserves in the Permian Basin. Soon other major oil companies were attracted to the region, and over time it became the largest oil producing area in the United States.

Those who took part in drilling Santa Rita No. 1 continued to be involved in the regional oil business. Locklin spent the rest of his life working in the Permian Basin's oilfields. Cromwell later became the Drilling Superintendent for Texon and, prior to his untimely death in 1931, was largely responsible for discovering the deeper pay zone in the Big Lake Field. Pickrell and Krupp ended their association in 1929, when Texon sold its controlling interest in the Big Lake Field for $9.5 million.

Not only does the memory of Santa Rita No. 1 live on, but the actual equipment that drilled the well has also been preserved. In 1940, through the efforts of several members of the Texas State Historical Association and UT alumnae, that material was salvaged and put into storage in Austin. It languished there until 1958, when a complete restoration of the drilling rig was rebuilt on the main campus of the University of Texas. The well itself continued to produce until 1990 when, after sixty-seven years of operation, it was taken out of service and plugged.

But when it is all said and done, perhaps the greatest service Santa Rita No. 1 has made for Texas lies in the realm of education. Its unique location on the University Lands made it the first oil well to contribute royalties to the PUF. Although that August 1923 payment only amounted to the paltry sum of $516.63, within two years it grew to $2,000 per day. Over a hundred years, it has continued its upward spiral. So it was that a cast of unlikely characters operating in an inhospitable and isolated environment fanned a tiny spark into the blaze that would ultimately change the lives of generations of Texans for the better.

Best, in Reagan County, about 1924.
Courtesy of Portal to Texas History

3   EXPANDING THE BASIN (1923–1930)

WHEN THE BIG LAKE BOOM took off late in 1923, the primary access to the oilfield was the struggling Kansas City, Mexico, and Orient Railway, generally referred to as the Orient Railway. It normally ran a mixed train of a couple of boxcars and a flatcar or two plus a passenger car every day or two from San Angelo to Fort Stockton and points west. As oilfield activity picked up, rail traffic grew by leaps and bounds, with long strings of cars loaded with tons of supplies. The little siding at Best expanded tremendously as huge pipe yards were built and warehouses proliferated.

To serve the large numbers of workers arriving, a small tent-and-shack town called Santa Rita developed at the well site, but it disappeared within a year to be replaced by Best. Best became a bustling boom town with a somewhat dubious reputation. It was the first of several new towns that sprang up over the next four or five years to serve the oilfield workers.

For a year or so following the Santa Rita discovery, there was a frenzy of leasing across the region. Beyond those involved in the expansion of the Big Lake Field, the only people making any money were state administrators and ranchers, who were getting top dollar for their leases. Lease buyers spread across the region in droves, and scores of isolated drilling sites began to pop up everywhere. They were small, self-contained camps consisting of a drilling rig and associated storage facilities along with some tents and skid-mounted shotgun houses for sleeping and cooking that served the eight to ten workers operating the drill site. The houses were very much like those that existed during the drilling of Santa Rita No. 1, but they were better equipped.

Traveling around the area to serve its burgeoning activity continued to present a problem. A good example of the difficulties is explained in a 1970 interview with Harold T. Morely, who described a 1925 trip from Hobbs, New Mexico, to Big Lake across the heart of the Permian Basin:

> On the way down there we had one spare tire and we went from Hobbs across the desert to Midland on those sand roads and I think we spent about half the time pulling mesquite thorns out of the tires. It took a long time because we had trouble keeping those five tires full of air. Well, it was a desert. When you got away from a settlement it was sand and mesquite. Of course there were cattle trails, but you could go down a road and you would have a turn—there would be a fork in the road. We finally decided that they always came back together. One road went around the hill this way and the other went that way, but they came back together so it got so it didn't make any difference which fork you took.

On another occasion Morely made a 150-mile trip from Midland to Abilene over a "good graded road" that lasted nine hours. He recalled that it was a good idea to take two people when traveling by automobile anywhere in the Permian Basin in those days. One did the driving, while the other helped fix the numerous flat tires caused by all the thorny vegetation, although that second rider also had to dig the car out of the seemingly endless series of soft sand beds.

The first successful wildcat well drilled after the opening of the Big Lake Field lay some fifty miles to the west in Upton County, population 253. Most people lived in Rankin, which, being the only town in the county, served as the county seat. The action began in September 1925, when Baker No. 1, drilled four miles north of the Orient Railway by Fort Worth wildcatters George B. McCamey and J. P. Johnson, blew in to spark the second oil boom in the Permian Basin. By early 1926, at least seven major oil companies were leasing properties in the area, and hordes of workers were pouring in.

When McCamey and Johnson first began their drilling operation, the Orient Railway established a siding near their well site. McCamey parked several boxcars there to store supplies.

One had a huge, crudely painted sign on its side that read "McCamey." Business was conducted from that location for a time. Soon a townsite company was organized, the name McCamey was adopted, and by March 1926 McCamey, Texas, had a post office. During its first six months of existence, the town is estimated to have had 10,000 residents. It had all the characteristics of an oil boom with a decided lack of amenities, It did not even have a water well for the first year or so. Water had to be brought from Alpine in railroad tank cars. Needless to say, in keeping with the stereotypes of many preceding oil boom towns, in those first days the community suffered from a considerable amount of lawless activity from the young, single oilfield workers who were always the first on the scene.

In March 1926, as the McCamey boom was hitting its stride, another successful wildcat well blew in to open another field in Crane County thirty miles to the north. With a population of only 37 lonely souls, the county had no towns at all. It had been formed in 1887, but a lack of population delayed its organization until 1927, after the oil boom had attracted enough people to plat the town of Crane. By the time Crane was built, the county boasted a population of 6,000, 4,500 of whom lived in the town, although it was not actually incorporated until the early 1930s.

Meanwhile, another boom was in the making some twenty miles southeast of McCamey, just west of the Pecos River in far southeastern Pecos County. It was an extremely isolated area where, back in 1915, Ira Yates had established a cattle ranch. Yates was struggling financially in 1923 when he learned of the activity going on in the Big Lake Field, so he contacted Levi Smith with the Benedum organization about leasing some of his more than 20,000-acre property. He finally persuaded them to take 8,000 acres where, over the next couple of years, they drilled four dry holes before bringing in the first producer on October 26, 1926.

Yates' ranch house, located near the west bank of the Pecos River, soon became a very popular place, with lease hounds lining up to get a chance to part with their money. Legend has it that Ira did all his business from a rocking chair on his front porch, where on one memorable day he signed $180,000 worth of leases. Almost overnight boomers poured in and created the short-lived town of Red Barn right across the Pecos River from the Yates home. It immediately became such a lawless place that within a few months Yates donated some property a short distance up the river, and a town was platted there and named Iraan. The name combines Yates's and his wife's first names, Ira and Ann.

The Yates Field's 15,000 acres proved to be unusual in many ways. The wells were all relatively shallow, all being in the 1,000-foot range, allowing them to be drilled with portable cable tool units that negated the expensive rig building process. But the most important aspect was the production rate. Most of the wells produced in the range of 1,000 barrels per day, with many going over 4,000 and one exceeding 8,000. Another auxiliary development associated with the Yates boom was that Rankin, twenty miles to the north on the Orient Railway, also

Crane, in Crane County, on January 7, 1927.
Courtesy of Portal to Texas History

Ira Yates' ranch in Pecos County in the 1920s.
Courtesy of Portal to Texas History

Iraan, near Ira Yates' ranch, in 1928.
Courtesy of the Portal to Texas History

boomed as the primary supply point to the Yates Field.

The three big booms at McCamey, Crane, and Iraan, coming on the heels of the opening of the Big Lake Field, led to further expansion through numerous smaller discoveries of oil in that southern part of the Permian Basin south of the T&P Railway (present day Interstate 20). The expansion lasted until the early 1930s. Drilling was spurred on by spectacular successes, and exploratory wells cropped up across the area farther to the north. The first major success north of the T&P Railway came in mid-summer of 1926. On July 16, about twenty miles north of the T&P amidst the sandhills of Winkler County, population 81, Hendrick No. 1 was completed by Fort Worth businessman Roy A. Westbrook. Due to the isolated location, extreme difficulty of transport across a sand-hill-covered landscape, and the total absence of a pipeline to transport production, a boom did not immediately develop. But serious development began in 1927, and within a year more than 200 rigs were running in the Hendrick Field.

Almost from its beginning, Hendrick Field attracted numerous townsite developers. Places like Brookfield, Cheyenne, and Tulsa cropped up, and by mid-1927 the Wink Townsite Company established Wink some seven miles south of the county seat of Kermit. Wink quickly became the focus of the developing boom, and the others faded from the scene. Of all the Permian Basin's towns, Wink had the most notorious reputation for lawlessness. As it happened, Wink's beginning coincided with the Texas Rangers' declaration of martial law at Borger in the Panhandle where a well-organized criminal element controlled that boom town. Consequently, most of the Borger group simply relocated their bootlegging, prostitution, and gambling activities to Wink, where they thrived for a time. The estimated population of Wink fluctuated wildly, but the official census in 1930 listed it at 6,000, although by that time the Hendrick Field was in a steep decline due to water encroachment in the wells.

Logistics for the booming Hendrick Field were a veritable nightmare. The closest supply point to the field was tiny Pyote, twenty miles to the south on the T&P Railway. Hauling freight across the sandhills was out of the question for trucks, so the work was done by teamsters. Wagons with twenty- and thirty-horse hitches became commonplace, but freight stacked up along the sidings at Pyote faster than it could be moved. Nevertheless, for the next two years workers streamed into the town, which some estimated reached a population of 20,000. Finally, in 1929 transport problems were solved when a rail line was built from the T&P at Monahans north to Wink. Over the next few years, Pyote returned to its former state of a couple of hundred or so residents.

During the mid to late 1920s, discoveries were definitely trending northward in the Permian Basin, and the Basin's boundaries were becoming more and more clearly defined. Along its west side, more discoveries began to develop in New Mexico near the Texas state line in Eddy and Lea counties. Some minor wells were drilled near Artesia in Eddy County as early as 1923, although the area did not gain any momentum until the mid-1930s. Meanwhile, to the north near the tiny town of Jal, in Lea County, on November 1, 1927, the Texas Company (Texaco) brought in Rhodes No. 1 as a good producer. The next year, on June 22, another well blew in at 90 million cubic feet of gas. Those discoveries caused a considerable boom for a short while and completely overwhelmed Jal. In the same year, 1928, following the short-lived Jal boom, another producing well blew in near Eunice, also in Lea County, which grew from a few hundred residents to 5,500 in a little over a year.

Perhaps the largest boom developed near Hobbs, in Lea County, beginning in 1927 when the Midwest Oil Company drilled a big producing well. The following year a refinery was built in the vicinity, and in 1929 Hobbs was incorporated. At its peak, the town had an estimat-

Hendrick Field in Winkler County about 1928.
Courtesy of Portal to Texas History

Wink, in Winkler County, about 1928.
Courtesy of Portal to Texas History

ed population of 12,000, although by 1930 the official population was 3,000. Hobbs quickly became the center of oil and gas production in Lea County, which itself was destined to become the leading petroleum producing county in New Mexico.

So it was that in the ten years between 1920, when the first successful Permian Basin oil well was drilled on its eastern flank near Westbrook in Mitchell County, and 1930, when oil was being produced in southeastern New Mexico on its western edge, the outlines of the greatest oil and gas producing region in the United States became much more clearly defined. Thousands of wells drilled during that decade provided significant geological information, much of it collected by the Bureau of Economic Geology at UT, greatly expanding the knowledge of the Basin's subsurface. That growing body of information brought a more precise scientific methodology for predicting future successful drilling locations. Although the information had long-term implications for the area, the most immediate obvious result was the economic importance of the phenomenal growth of oil and gas production in the region. Practically all that growth can be traced directly the completion of Santa Rita No. 1 in 1923, which sparked the expansion of serious oil and gas activity to the west and the north.

During the 1920 to 1930 period, oil and gas development also brought significant changes to the Permian Basin in population growth and social orientation. Before the huge influx of oil workers began, the region was occupied almost exclusively by a small, isolated ranching population. By 1930, an overwhelming number of residents were involved in the petroleum industry. Along with them came the establishment of new towns, including Best, Texon, McCamey, Iraan, Wink, and a dozen or so short-lived ones like Santa Rita, Red Barn, and Cheyenne.

Getting an accurate accounting of the population explosion is difficult, given the chaotic nature of oil booms. When affairs were at their height, with drilling going full blast, large pipelines being built, tank farms under construction, and the supply chain bustling, there was a tremendous amount of temporary labor in the area. As the boom faded, the temporary workers left, work and life settled into a more normal operating mode, and a permanent population emerged. For example, McCamey at the height of its boom in 1926 was estimated at 10,000, Pyote at 20,000 during the opening of the Hendrick Field, and Hobbs at 12,000 during the height of its boom. However, the 1930 census shows a different picture, with both McCamey and Hobbs in the 3,000 range and Pyote at only a few hundred people.

The United States census indicates that at the time oil was discovered in the Permian Basin in 1920, the twenty core counties of the Basin had a population of 44,656, which in just ten years expanded almost threefold to 126,408. The change was proportionately greater in the area south of the T&P, where the original discoveries lay. Its 6,297 citizens in 1920 grew to 21,112 by 1930, for an increase of 235 percent. North of that line there were 38,359 residents in 1920, which increased to slightly under 100,000 by 1930, or a growth of 161 percent. But considering the large size of the region, all that population change still left the Basin a very lightly populated area.

The successful development of oil and gas in the Permian Basin changed the nature of life there, and it had an even greater impact on higher education in the state of Texas at large. When Santa Rita No. 1 blew in, right in the middle of the University Lands, finance for higher education in the Lone Star State changed forever. In 1921, additional land had been purchased adjacent to the original UT campus for a planned expansion, but the legislature refused to appropriate any funds to build on the property. In 1931, using the PUF as collateral, UT issued bonds and began building. Over the next several years, many of the central campus structures were razed and replaced. The central feature of the transformed campus became the 1934 Tower, a landmark which has become perhaps the most recognized symbol of the university. Along with growth in the physical plant, there was a significant expansion of course work, including the founding of the Department of Petroleum Engineering. It graduated its first two students in 1931 and by the 1940s was recognized as one of the largest programs in the nation.

Following the initial discovery of oil on University Lands in 1923, significant public debate emerged about reserving all the oil and gas income to UT. As a result, in 1931 the Texas Legislature amended the law to allow TAMU to share in the distribution of the funds. Since then, the annual allocation of funding from the PUF toward higher education has been divided, with the ratio set at one-third for TAMU and two-thirds for UT. Over the years, the endowment has grown to become one of the largest in the nation.

The Permian Basin oil and gas industry momentum of the 1920s significantly slowed at the beginning of the 1930s when it became clear that drilling was moving northward from those first discoveries. Two other factors were involved in the slowdown. First, the Great Depression that curtailed all economic activity in the nation was beginning to have a definite impact on the oil and gas industry. Second, and more immediate, was the 1930 discovery of a massive oilfield in East Texas that drew large numbers of workers away from the Permian Basin.

That East Texas discovery was characterized by thousands of small leases from small farmers. In this situation, operators produced as much as they could to assure that their oil leases remained economically viable. Unbridled oil production ensued, at one point driving the price of oil down to ten cents per barrel. It took most of the decade of the 1930s for the Basin to gradually bring itself back into a position of increasing financial prosperity and a growing population.

Texon, in Reagan County, in the 1920s.
Courtesy of the Portal to Texas History

4 A ROOF OVER THEIR HEADS (1923-1930)

THAT LARGE INFLUX OF PEOPLE into the Permian Basin presented a real housing problem. They came in basically two waves. The first is that overwhelming group at the beginning of a boom, about which so much has been written concerning their rough and rowdy nature. The second was composed of those who were there for the long haul, of whom little notice has been made. Perhaps lurid headlines have as much to do with this as anything. Murder and mayhem are much more exciting than building a stable, long-lasting lifestyle.

The character of boom towns varied considerably depending upon several elements. Generally, those that existed prior to the boom often had an existing city government and law enforcement system that could control people. Those that did not exist prior to the boom had a tendency toward a more chaotic existence. Regardless of the nature of boom-generated unstable social conditions, they generally only existed for a short while until the peak of the boom passed.

The first of the pre-existing towns in the Permian Basin to experience the change was Big Lake, located on the Orient Railway just twelve miles east of Santa Rita No. 1. At the time of the discovery of oil, it was a little cattle-shipping community numbering 100 souls.

Over the next few years that number grew to 2,000, who supported several new businesses. Given its distance from the center of the action, Big Lake did not attract significant numbers of the boomer types. Instead, it became the temporary headquarters for oil company men bent on leasing property and establishing operations.

Big Lake had only one small hotel with a limited capacity that was entirely inadequate to accommodate the business. Accordingly, oilman Hal A. Hedberg and Paul Doran bought a hotel at Fort Stockton and had it dismantled, moved to Big Lake, and rebuilt. That two-story, fifty-room building filled so quickly that they double rented rooms and still had to turn customers away. With business so good, within months they built another hotel, which also filled to capacity. Ultimately, the usual wild and woolly town of Best, at the site of the discovery, appeared, and the partners built a third hotel. The three operated at full capacity for about three years until the boom subsided. At that point Hedberg and Doran dismantled the original hotel and moved it to Pyote, where a new massive boom was underway. Although hotel construction at Big Lake illustrates the sudden increase in population associated with the boom, generally the traditional temporary shoddy housing and social chaos that has been associated with boom towns did not develop there.

Best, where Hedberg and Doran built their third hotel, was an entirely different situation. As Hedberg described it in a 1970 interview, "It was a smaller town and it consisted of mostly oilfield workers and the type of people who follow the boom: boomer types, racketeers, dope peddlers, bootleggers, and what have you." That situation hampered the ability of the Big Lake Oil Company to hire competent and stable employees, so the company created a unique, for the oilfield, solution to the problem: a company town named Texon.

Traditionally the term "company town" is associated with extractive industries such as mining, in which employees are held in a sort of debt bondage. In Texas the town of Thurber, in Erath County, comes to mind as a classic example. At Thurber, the company held title to all the land and owned all the businesses, churches, and schools, as well as the houses where all employees lived. They were paid with scrip, redeemable at the company store. That concept did not transfer well to the oil and gas industry. Unlike a mining town like Thurber, where the workers lived in one spot for years, oilfield labor had a much more fluid situation that peaked during short-lived booms and quickly waned as a field settled into steady production. The establishment of Texon refutes the commonly held idea that a company town is a bad thing that keeps employees in a sort of bondage. Texon sprang more from the owners' paternalistic desire to provide a better life for their workers, which in turn gave the company a cadre of loyal employees that translated into a more efficient work force.

Texon began with Levi Smith, vice president and general manager of the Big Lake Oil Company. He was so appalled by the chaotic conditions at Best and Santa Rita that he decided to build a town whose residents would be restricted to company employees. He reasoned that by providing good living conditions, he would attract family-oriented workers who would stay with the company, rather than the usual single men who tended to follow the booms. He was convinced that concept would translate into a stable workforce and a more efficient and profitable operation.

The site Smith chose for Texon lay about fourteen miles west of Big Lake, barely outside the two-mile by four-mile production field and just south of the Kansas City, Mexico, and Orient Railway tracks. Between 1924 and 1926 Texon, named in honor of the company that had brought in Santa Rita No. 1, became a reality. It was an oasis of calm and refuge amid the rough and tumble of the full-fledged oil boom going on in that part of West Texas. Indeed, Texon was widely touted in publications of the day as a fine example of a well-ordered community that exemplified the benevolent nature of oil companies toward their employees.

Early in 1924, amid the frenzied drilling program of the boom, Smith started building Texon with the installation of supply warehouses, pipe yards, and workshops on the railroad side of town. That was quickly followed by construction of a series of two-bedroom residences designed to house administrative personnel along Main Street. Immediately across from those first houses, he erected several buildings designed to be rented for a variety of businesses. At the same time, he built a huge number of one-bedroom shotgun houses for the hourly employees that ultimately made up the larger portion of the town.

In the early days of Texon, utilities were at a premium. Although gas was piped in from the field for heating and cooking purposes, it was a while before a generator was installed to provide electricity to homes and businesses. Water was even more difficult to obtain, and the precious fluid was either delivered by tank trucks or fetched from a centrally located water tank. In those early years, the company provided two large bath houses, one for men and one for women, near the center of town.

By the time construction ended in 1926, electrical power was available, and water was piped into all the houses of its 1,200 residents. Businesses had cropped up by then in all the rental spaces along Main Street. At its peak, Texon had a café, drugstore grocery store, dry goods store, boarding house, filling station, movie theater, a barber shop, and several other retail accoutrements of a town. Additionally, it had a post office, community church, hospital, and elementary school. The school served children from the first through the sixth grades, while those older were bused to schools in Big Lake. Recreation also played a large role in the life of the town as evidenced by the existence of a company-built golf course complete with "greens" of oiled sand in lieu of grass, tennis courts, a swimming pool, a club house, and a baseball stadium.

The baseball stadium is particularly interesting because Smith, who was an avid fan, organized a semi-pro baseball team to play there. The summer of 1925 brought the completion of the baseball field, and the following year a five-hundred-seat grandstand was added. Although originally called the Big Lake Oil Company Oilers, the team soon became the Texon Oilers. The roster was filled by former college athletes as well as seasoned semi-pro players hired on a full-time work/play basis. In 1929, the company began hosting a huge annual Labor Day barbeque and baseball game for all employees and friends. The Texon Oilers had a successful run in various West Texas leagues through the decade of the 1930s. However, with the waning of oil production and the decline of the town's population, the team was disbanded at the beginning of the 1940s, just as World War II began.

During its heyday, Texon experienced considerable competition among company employees to acquire one of the rental houses and escape the primitive living conditions in the field. Rental for homes varied widely from $4 per month for the little one-bedroom shotgun houses to as much as $35 for one of the larger two-bedroom houses along Main Street, which were usually reserved for management personnel. Also, among the town's residents were two or three African American families, an uncommon situation in the oilfields of the day. Their men were hired to perform general maintenance on the various town buildings.

By the beginning of the 1940s, Texon's population began to slip in a direct relationship to the decline of production of the Big Lake Field. Some employees were transferred to other locations, some retired, and some just left as the job market dried up. During the first years of the 1950s, the population of Texon had fallen from well over 1,000 to less than 500. In 1956, ownership of the town passed to the Plymouth Oil Company, and the population continued to decline. Then, in 1962 the Marathon Oil Company purchased the property and discontinued its maintenance. By 1986, the post office had closed.

In 1962, when Marathon discontinued maintaining the town, those still living there, along with others long gone from the community, organized an annual reunion held over Labor Day weekend. It was reminiscent of what they had done in years gone by, when the company hosted a barbeque and baseball game. Later, the reunion moved to the first weekend in June, and eventually it was only held every other year. As late as the early 2000s, the event attracted more than one hundred visitors, but interest waned until 2014, when the last reunion was held on the site. Today there are no structures left on the site of Texon, but its memory lives on as the example of the only true company town established in the oilfields of Texas.

The reality of other oilfield boom towns was a far cry from the situation at Texon. Its residents were for the most part young single men drawn to the good wages associated with following booms and working for contractors. There were a sprinkling of oil company men serving the interests of their employers along with fair number of family men also working for contractors. A good example of one of the latter is Joseph Grabble, who decided to follow the booms without subjecting his family to the associated hardships. In a 1970s interview he recalled, "I never cashed a check. I sent all my checks to my wife and she would send me money. Whenever I needed clothes, she knew my sizes, I'd tell her what I needed and she would ship them to me." Of course, there were a large number of businesspeople operating cafés, boarding houses, lumber yards, and all those things necessary for a town to exist. But always hovering out on the edges like some dark cloud was that criminal element, preying on those who were trying to earn an honest living.

Before the boom towns developed, given the isolated nature of those first drill sites, tents were the most common shelter available. Normally a drilling crew would be hired for the duration of the job, which always lasted several weeks and could drag on for months. To insure keeping a work force during the drilling process, the crews were not paid until the well was completed. Room and board were part of the deal. A drill site would normally include a cluster of tents composed of sleeping quarters, a cooking/dining tent, and possibly a headquarters tent for conducting business matters. After the well was completed or abandoned, the crew was paid, and the tents were packed and moved to another location. Depending upon the circumstance, the hands either went to the new location or sought other employment. In either case, they often took their hefty payment to the nearest boom town and kicked up their heels.

Once a field was assured of strong development, mobile crews arrived to build various projects necessary to store and transport the oil. They produced veritable cities of tents that were used to house those temporary workers. The most obvious of the workers were the pipeliners. Long pipelines required three large crews consisting of a hundred or more each who used large tent camps that moved along the right-of-way. The first camp was for right-of-way clearance and trenching, the second for pipe laying, and the last for backfilling and cleanup. Others, like those building the huge, riveted tanks of 55,000-barrel capacity or larger for the tank farms, often lived in tent cities until the work was completed. Then there were teamsters, who arrived with thousands of horses and mules that were stabled away from the towns; teamsters also lived in tents.

Just as tents were the housing of choice at drill sites and for those workers involved in the more mobile occupations, they were also usually the first type of housing in the various boom towns. For example, McCamey started as a railroad siding where George B. McCamey put his name on a boxcar to indicate where to unload his supplies. Teamsters who unloaded the freight cars stayed nearby in a cluster of tents. Almost all the early boom towns started that way, with a cluster of

Early housing at Goldsmith, in Ector County, in 1937.
Courtesy of Portal to Texas History

tents located at some location central to the field being developed. Although they were generally referred to as "ragtowns" or "shacktowns," there was a certain order to how boom towns developed. Once the town became a reality, housing began to take on a more permanent nature. If the tents remained, they became modified into half-walled structures with wooden floors and wooden siding rising to about four feet, providing considerably more stability and insulation. Frame structures with gypsum board on the inside and tarpaper exteriors were also widely used. But the most common type of living space was the shotgun house.

When the topic of conversation turns to early oilfield boom town housing, the most often mentioned structure is the shotgun house. It is always described as a small two- or three-room house with the rooms arranged in a straight line, one behind the other. Its name is supposedly derived from the fact that if a shotgun was fired through the front door, the charge would pass through the house and out the back door. Perhaps that is as good a description as any, but the history of that ubiquitous oil patch institution is a long and interesting story.

According to architectural historians, it had its beginnings in Africa, was moved to Haiti by slaves, and finally to New Orleans, where during the nineteenth century it became one of the most popular housing styles among the working classes. It required no drawn plans, was inexpensive to build, and could be constructed with almost any readily available building materials by workers of limited experience. Further, the shotgun required a small footprint and had excellent air circulation, making it ideal for living in the hot southern and southwestern parts of the country. Participants in the Permian Basin booms in the 1920s and early1930s all comment upon the many rows of shotgun houses in those towns.

The lumber companies, which were among the first to arrive at any boom town, were quick to take advantage of that situation. Their standard product was a ten-foot by twenty-foot structure generally called "the boxcar" that sold for $80 and could be erected in one day by an experienced carpenter using the pre-cut lumber provided by the lumber yard. They even provided a ten-foot by thirty-foot deluxe version. These house kits were replicated by the hundreds when the booms were at their height. Vacancies were so scarce during those days that those small inadequate structures regularly rented for as much as $75 per month. Any enterprising landlord could easily recoup his investment within a month or two.

Living conditions in the little houses were far from luxurious. There was no electricity, gas, or running water. Homes, as well as businesses, were lit by kerosene lanterns and used water from questionable sources which left much to be desired. In general, the people living there experienced very unsanitary conditions, prices were exorbitant, and there was a high rate of crime and violence. That was in part because, during their first years, all boom towns were characterized by any number of dance halls, drinking emporiums, and houses of ill repute.

Just like Smith at Texon, many officials for large oil companies struggled with the problem of attracting and keeping stable, family-oriented employees who could work hard under stressful conditions. The solution was twofold. The first task was to avoid creating an unsavory boom town. Second, given that so much of the actual work activity was far from any town, it was necessary to provide adequate living conditions in isolated locations. The companies' approach was to develop an oilfield "camp" system.

The use of camps was not a new concept to the oilfield. Camps can be differentiated from company towns primarily because the former did not have retail districts or a post office to identify them. They were first extensively used in downstream operations in the Gulf Coast region to house various refinery and petrochemical workers and in midstream pipeline operations at the pump and compressor stations. By the time large-scale oil and gas operations moved into the Permian Basin in the mid-1920s, the companies had refined the camps considerably, and they proved to be the perfect solution for providing their workers with good living conditions. Because of the underpopulated and harsh nature of the Permian Basin landscape, oilfield camps became in large part a unifying social aspect of the region.

The hundreds of camps made up of solid, well-built homes ran the gamut in size. Many were not camps at all but a multitude of widely scattered individual lease houses built to house pumpers and their families while they maintained the pumps and storage facilities on individual leases. Then there were small pipeline camps situated at the various pump and compressor stations on a host of major pipelines that crisscrossed the region. But the most numerous were larger production camps, many in close proximity to the newly built boom towns. The production camps contained major supply-storage facilities and workshops in addition to administrative offices and living quarters. Taken as a whole, the camps in the Permian Basin ranged in size from a dozen or fewer to as many as a hundred homes scattered everywhere across the region.

As an example of the magnitude of an operation, the town of Crane had twenty-five camps in close proximity to it. The largest and most luxurious was the Gulf Oil Company's McElroy Camp. It boasted 65 houses, six 30-room bunk houses, a hospital, a swimming pool, tennis courts, and a club house in addition to an extensive complex of administrative, repair, and storage facilities. Humble Oil & Refining Company had both a pipeline camp and a production camp, Cities Service Company had one, Magnolia Petroleum Company had one, Phillips Petroleum Company had one, and the list goes on and on. In the case of Crane, which maintained a population of between 3,000 and 4,000 that waxed and waned according to oilfield activity, the surrounding camp population remained about the same size and provided reliable economic support to the town. The same could be said of all the camps surrounding the boom towns in the region, particularly newly established communities like McCamey, Iraan, and Wink.

Although the oil patch, both then and now, has a very egalitarian attitude among those working in the industry, there is a distinct although subtle social divide between the contractors and company people. Nowhere was this more apparent than with the development of the camp system. There, company people were physically separated from contractors, who lived exclusively in the towns. Although many of the camp dwellers had worked as contractors for years, as they grew older and acquired families, they tended to gravitate toward the more settled lifestyle and regular paycheck provided by employment with the large companies.

Additionally, the camp system provided a strong program of bonding the employees into a cohesive group. For example, the larger camps usually had an annual picnic and banquet-style gatherings on various holidays such as the Fourth of July and Christmas. Games were played, gifts were given, and various employee awards were announced. They also developed a variety of sports-related activities such as tennis and golf tournaments, and some developed a baseball league for which the various camps fielded teams. The baseball league, much like the situation at Texon, became such a highly competitive situation that college players were recruited as workers, but their main duties lay with their ability on the baseball diamond.

Education was another aspect supported by the camp system. Given the massive support the oil companies were pumping into the local tax base, they played an important role in supporting the school systems in the Permian Basin. Although none of the camps provided schools, all the school districts developed excellent bus systems, assuring that all oil-camp children, who provided at least half the school

Gulf Oil rigs in Crane County in the late 1920s.
Courtesy of Portal to Texas History

population in those early days, could attend the nearest school.

The camp system worked admirably from the time of its introduction in the early 1920s until the late 1950s. It remained an integral part of the Permian Basin lifestyle as the focus of field activity moved further north toward the Midland/Odessa area and beyond to the northern limits of the Basin during the 1930s and 1940s. But like all things in the petroleum industry, it fell victim to changing technology. By the late 1950s a couple of generations of oil patch people had grown up in the camps and had become accustomed to that lifestyle. Then a series of circumstances brought an end to the camps. The first was that improved roads and general improvement in the means of transportation allowed workers to live farther from their work. That made it unnecessary for them to live close to the job site, a main concern in the formation of the camp system. The regional towns had long since outgrown the rough-and-tumble reputation of their early days, which had been another reason to establish the camps. The basic needs for the camps were gone, and so in light of the considerable financial burden of maintaining them, oil companies eliminated the system. Starting in the late 1950s and continuing into the early 1960s, the last camps were dismantled, and workers moved into local towns. By the end of the 1960s, company camps were a thing of the past.

That change was a traumatic event for many of those who had spent twenty or more years living in a highly subsidized situation, where the only housing expense was a small monthly fee. The companies realized that and tried to make the transition as painless as possible. They allowed the residents to purchase their house for a low price, often as low as one dollar, and move it to the town of their choice. The only real expense to the employee was in moving, buying a lot in town, and getting the house situated in its new home. Nevertheless, dislocated workers sometimes showed considerable animosity. They suddenly had taxes and utility bills to pay, homes and yards to maintain, and all the other expenses associated with home ownership. For many who had spent their working lives with only a pittance spent on housing, there was bitterness toward their employers. With time the hard feelings dissipated, to be replaced with fond memories of good times spent with their fellow workers. In some cases, oil companies donated camp property for civic improvements. The Gulf camp at Crane and another at Andrews were given to the respective cities and transformed into city parks. But most were cleared of all structures, and all that is left are some scraggly trees to mark where houses once stood.

Perhaps the most important thing that remains from the camp system is its contribution to the strong bond that exists among the oilfield people of the Permian Basin. In the United States, there are few if any geographical areas the size of the Permian Basin focused on a single industry. Within a decade or so of the drilling of Santa Rita No. 1, the oil industry had totally eclipsed the region's ranching economy, increased the sparse population more than threefold, and provided the foundation for future growth of higher education in the state. In addition, all the expansion sparked the growth of a distinct oilfield culture that grew out of the act of finding ways to put a roof over their heads.

In terms of oilfield culture, it can generally be said the people all came for financial gain. There were the young, adventurous types that made the boom towns boom. There were the serious businessmen, who established numerous small oil-related firms, and large oil company executives trying to establish stability. There were the thousands of hard-working contractors and company employees who came for good wages, and there was even the criminal element. They all played their part in creating the distinct social and cultural norms that came to identify residents of that region.

Many came but not all stayed. Some were overwhelmed by the harsh nature of the landscape, while others were repelled by the unsettled and often dangerous nature of the work. Those soon returned whence they came. Those who remained formed the core of the people who made it happen. By nature, they were an independent lot looking for opportunity: "With a little luck I too can become an oil baron." That independence manifested itself in many ways. For example, labor unions are a rarity in the oil patch because the transient nature of employment by contractors fostered an attitude of "I was looking for a job when I got this one" or "I think I'll just whip the driller and walk off the job." Good pay and a place to live satisfied most company workers. Besides, both groups generally viewed labor unions as just another boss to endure.

Most of all, an egalitarian state of mind developed, fostered by the bond of everybody being involved in the same business and having the same experiences. From the inside it is "we are all in this together doing something worthwhile," but from the outside the reaction is "why in the world do those people act that way."

Nitroglycerin drop goes wrong at Skelly-Amerada University No. 1 in Ector County on April 27, 1930.
Courtesy of Portal to Texas History

5 THE WORK THEY DID AND HOW IT CHANGED (1923–1930)

AT THE TIME SANTA RITA NO. 1 was drilled, the nature of oilfield work was little changed from its 1901 beginnings in Texas. The technology was both labor intensive and relatively inefficient, and scientific knowledge on how to recognize subsurface petroleum reserves was in a state of flux. The oil business was ripe for change during the first years of the Permian Basin's existence. But as any old timer would tell you, "It is hard to convince those old-time oilfield hands to change," so progress was often slow.

First was the question of just what comprised the Permian Basin and where, within its confines, was the oil. The main difficulty was the absence of surface geological indicators to work from in that flat and relatively featureless region. The initial studies done prior to 1920 by the Bureau of Economic Geology at UT had sparked the drilling of Santa Rita No. 1. These surveys were conducted around the periphery of the Basin, where outcroppings indicated the likelihood of a huge, deeply buried basin with formations capable of containing petroleum. However, that early information was very general in nature.

Santa Rita No. 1's success was a hit or miss, wildcat-type activity. Most of the discoveries immediately following it were of the same general type. Gradually over time scientific geological data obtained from completed well logs provided a better understanding of the geology of the Permian Basin. But it was far from complete. The next step in gaining accurate geological forecasts and finding oil was the development of a practical reflective seismographic technology that could ascertain the location of likely oil- bearing formations. The process, developed in 1921, measured the intensity of vibrations created by dynamite blasts and reflected off of subsurface formations. Analysis of that data indicated where and at what depth various formations lay. Seismography was the perfect tool to predict likely drilling locations in the Permian Basin. Its first success in the area came in 1927 with the discovery well at Hobbs, New Mexico. After that, the use of geophysical detection technology, which oilfield people called "doodle-bugging," quickly came into general use throughout the Basin.

In concert with scientific developments helping identify likely drilling conditions, numerous improvements were made in actual well drilling. Perhaps the most important was the introduction of rotary drilling units to the Permian Basin. Although rotary drilling was first used at Corsicana in 1894 and later, beginning in 1901, in Gulf Coast fields, where it became the mainstay for drilling in those unconsolidated formations, the preferred type of drilling remained the cable tool percussion method. It had been used since the 1850s with very little technological improvement. Cable tools worked just as well as the rotaries in those early days when most wells never exceeded the 3,000- to 4,000-foot depth. Below that, they had problems.

Additionally, most of the cable tool drillers who had been imported from Pennsylvania and West Virginia had the reputation of being notoriously cantankerous individuals who opposed trying anything new. There was an intense rivalry between the cable tool and the rotary factions, and both spouted all kinds of reasons why their methods were better. Many of those discussions tended to get so downright heated that they often ended in physical confrontations and caused serious bodily harm. Needless to say, the two groups tended to frequent different drinking emporiums in order to avoid such encounters. Back then, a story circulated concerning a couple of cable tool drillers walking along a boom-town street one day when they spied a sign that read, "Rotary Club meets here at noon on Friday." One of them exclaimed, "Can you believe that? Those blankety-blanks even have their own club."

The drilling process began to change as geologists suggested that there were pay zones at deeper depths than the "big lime," as the old-time drillers called that 3,000- to 4,000-foot producing level. One of the first successes came in 1928 when an 8,000-foot well, the deepest in the Permian Basin at that time, was completed in the Big Lake Field, substantially increasing production there. It was drilled with a rotary rig utilizing a new steel derrick instead of the traditional wooden structure. Interestingly, the drilling superintendent overseeing the job for the Texon Oil and Land Company was Carl G. Cromwell, who had laboriously drilled Santa Rita No. 1 with a cable tool rig just five years before.

As Permian Basin oil discoveries continued northward, the well depths deepened until by the early 1930s cable tools became obsolete. Drilling at those greater depths brought associated changes to the process. Wooden construction produced a weaker derrick structure, and the stress exerted upon it in the drilling process caused it likely to be "pulled in" or collapse. Traditionalists claimed that they could listen to the creaking noises and judge how much stress was being exerted. They said that there was no such warning on steel derricks, which made them unsafe.

Many times, drilling crews rigged a homemade weight indicator by hanging a stand of pipe from the derrick and suspending it just twelve inches above the drilling floor. Drillers maintained that most derricks could stand up to eight inches of "squat." So, by watching their device, they were safe as long as it stayed four inches or more above the drilling floor. The traditionalists' methods became outdated around 1930, when weight indicators were invented to tell the driller exactly how much stress was being exerted.

Good engineering and common sense won out, and by around 1930 steel derricks became the standard. The 72-foot derrick used by cable tool rigs proved adequate as long as the rotaries were pulling doubles (two sections of twenty-foot-long drill pipe), but as wells grew deeper, and rigs began pulling "thribbles" (three sections) and even "foibles" (four), derricks became much taller to accommodate them. During that same time frame, more powerful internal combustion engines replaced the earlier steam engines. Blowout devices were installed to contain unexpected extreme gas pressures caused by drilling into gas pockets or to fix other situations that could cause a well to blow out and possibly be lost to explosion or fire. More efficient electrical generators lit the locations, and drilling mud pits dominated sites. Drilling bits were significantly improved, primarily changing from fish-tailed, spade shaped devices that scraped their way through the earth to roller-cone style bits that cut downward through the formation. All these engineering and mechanical changes created a faster and much more efficient drilling process.

Drilling personnel also changed. The cable tool or percussion method of essentially pounding a hole in the ground required a two-man crew consisting of a driller, who ran the operation, and a tool dresser or "toolie." A rotary operation required a five-man crew consisting of a driller, two floor hands, a derrick man, and a motor man. The majority of the rotary crews were a home-grown lot, mostly Texans who had started their careers on the rotaries. With all the change and innovation, the drillers, who in the past had little supervision and could be an autocratic lot, lost some of their independence. "Tool pushers" were put in charge of each rig to ensure the operation was properly progressing. The element that did not change, regardless of the type of rig used or who was in charge, was the twelve-hour work shift or "tour," pronounced "tower" in the oil patch, which ran from midnight to noon (graveyards) and from noon until midnight (daylights) or in some cases from 7 a.m. to 7 p.m. and 7 p.m. until 7 a.m., depending upon who was doing the assignments.

The change from wood to steel also affected the nature of rig building. The steel rigs were still built in segments, but they were bolted together instead of nailed. The big advantage was that the parts could be used repeatedly by simply dismantling derricks and rebuilding them elsewhere. Sometimes, if the terrain was level enough, the entire structure could even be skidded to its new drilling location. Thus, the traditional "forest of derricks" image disappeared from the oilfields.

As drilling spread across the Basin, transportation remained the basic problem that always confronted those doing the work. In the first decade of Permian Basin development, there were still no paved roads. Even though the main highway across the region from Abilene to El Paso added its last segment by 1927, it remained what was called an "improved road," essentially made of packed gravel, and it was not actually paved until 1940. In 1935 a graded caliche road was built south from Odessa to Crane and a few years later extended further south to McCamey, connecting the original southern portion of the Basin to the developing northern sector.

Within the oilfield, road building was a constant process, and dirt contractors became an essential part of the overall activity. Access roads to the drill sites and other locations were being constantly built. Those on relatively sound terrain were simply graded and covered with packed caliche. However, road construction in the sandier areas and especially in the shifting sandhills required considerably more work. Eventually, the most abundant resource came to the rescue. The sand was graded off as level as possible and stabilized with a coating of oil. It worked

Oil prospectors traveling in a 1925 Dodge automobile through Brewster County in 1927.
Courtesy of Portal to Texas History

admirably, although it required constant maintenance by adding oil and repacking the surface. Ultimately, thousands of miles of both oiled and caliche lease roads crisscrossed the Permian Basin, binding the oil-producing region together into a single, coordinated entity.

By the time the network of lease roads and roads between the various new oil towns was completed, the power and efficiency of motorized vehicular traffic had greatly improved and included the development of track-driven excavation and grading vehicles for dirt work. A big slowdown in West Texas oil and gas activity beginning in 1930 and lasting for most of the 1930s, caused by the Great Depression and government regulations intended to correct the decline in oil prices, marked the end of the colorful era of the teamsters and the beginning of internal combustion-engine power for exploiting the Basin.

Changing technology also revolutionized pipeline building during the era. The last major threaded pipeline built by huge gangs of workers was a 546-mile combination eight- and ten-inch line built by the Gulf Oil Company from Crane, in the Permian Basin, to Lufkin, in southeastern Texas, in 1927. By the time this job was completed, a new kind of welding was making important improvements in pipeline construction. Welders had traditionally used the oxyacetylene method, but as soon as portable generators became strong enough to supply the necessary voltage, the old method was supplanted by shielded electric or arc welding. That change by around 1930 negated the need for huge crews to screw pipes together. At the same time, track-driven mechanical ditchers dug trenches while track-driven, side-boom vehicles laid the pipe and bulldozer-type vehicles took over the backfill job. By the mid-1930s, the manpower need in pipelining had been reduced by approximately 75 percent, while the speed of laying pipe had increased from an average of three-quarters of a mile per day to four and one-half miles per day.

Welding affected almost every facet of oilfield work by the 1930s.

One trade that was particularly changed was tank-building. Before the introduction of arc welding, all of the huge 55,000-to more than 100,000-barrel tank-farm storage tanks were riveted. Riveting, much like pipelining, required huge crews of workers. After the first years of the 1930s, there were no more riveted tanks built in the Permian Basin. This did not affect the traditional part of the tank-building trade that continued to produce thousands of bolted-steel field tanks in the 250- to 1,000-barrel capacity or the occasional 5000- or 10,000-barrel pipeline vessels of the same type. However, one notable anomaly was associated with the larger storage vessels, and it was more an experiment than anything else. In the late 1920s there were two one-million-barrel earthen excavations built, one just south of McCamey, and another just east of Monahans. They were lined with poured concrete, but both were abandoned without being used. It appeared that the bottoms developed significant cracks before the concrete cured.

The shooting of oil wells, another common oilfield occupation in the Permian Basin, differed somewhat from its practice in other parts of the country. The common belief that oil wells are drilled into some type of "lake of oil," which simply gushes oil to the surface in a giant plume, is erroneous, to say the least. Generally, oil is trapped in tiny spaces in certain types of rocks, and the rate at which it seeps out is termed "porosity." The greater the porosity, the larger amount of oil produced, so it is necessary to fracture the stone at the bottom of the well to enhance production. The process by which this done is called "shooting," which in effect means exploding nitroglycerin in the well to fracture or "frac" the stone.

In the early days, nitroglycerin, or "nitro," was a liquid substance (a gel process was not developed until the 1940s) requiring a 28-pound-per-square-inch jolt for it to explode. After some unfortunate incidents, a federal regulation prohibited the transporting of nitro by rail. After that, for oilfield use it had to be manufactured in isolated locations very near the oilfield where it would be used. Fortunately, making nitro was a simple nitration process that required glycerin to be slowly added to a mixture of nitric and sulfuric acid. The resulting liquid was poured into 10-gallon-square metal cans weighing thirty-three pounds each. Those filled cans were taken from the nitration plant and stored in small wooden or corrugated metal sheds that held a thousand quarts each and stood some distance apart. Since nitro becomes very unstable if frozen or subjected to temperatures in excess of 118 Fahrenheit, it required constant, close observation.

What differentiated well shooting in West Texas from that of previous areas was the dense nature of the sandstone and limestone formations to be shot. In other areas, shoots seldom ranged over 100 quarts per shot, but in the Permian Basin it took several hundred to more than a thousand to achieve the same results. As a result, whereas shooters normally used heavy duty automobiles with well-padded compartments to transport nitro to the well site, they were forced to utilize small trucks to do the same work in the Permian Basin. Miraculously there were few recorded incidents of serious accidents associated with well shooting in the region.

Oil-well fires are an offshoot of well shooting that over time achieved something of a legendary status. To make it clear, fires were few and far between, and those who made it their occupation to put them out were only a handful of very specialized individuals. There were fires in the Permian Basin, but none were of the spectacular nature that required months of time and an enormous expenditure to resolve.

Oil-well fires are always caused by gas ignition. For that to happen, there must be two situations. First, there must be a specific ratio of gas to air for gas to explode or burn. Second, there must be some sort of ignition device. The problem is how to either keep the gas out of the ignition range or nullify the ignition source. It may sound easy, but it is not. In an untold number of cases, a blowout occurred that

Nitroglycerin trucks at R. H. Henderson, UT Well No. 2, in Crane County in March 1939.
Courtesy of Portal to Texas History

was quickly stopped by a pressure-control device called a blowout preventer or by shutting down any spark-producing devices until the flow could be capped. If by chance that failed and a fire erupted, it was necessary to disrupt the gas-to-air ratio to extinguish the fire. In the earliest days of the field, the practice was to set up a battery of steam generators and play steam on the wellhead until the fire went out. As a last resort, a nitro blast would be produced at the wellhead, temporarily disrupting the gas-to-air ratio and extinguishing the blaze. No matter what is done, the central object is to cap the well and stop the gas and oil discharge. A good rule of thumb for drillers is to eliminate possible ignition devices such as glowing metal, sparks, or any other likely sources. In some cases, fires have been extinguished and then reignited on purpose to allow a continued flow of gas into the atmosphere while another method was being devised to shut off the flow. In short, what looks spectacular is not always the most important aspect of a situation.

The first years of the development of oil production in the Permian Basin came at a time when increasing technological change was providing a host of opportunities that heralded a new day in the oil patch of West Texas. The original and ongoing challenge of traveling in that the harsh landscape was brought under control through a better transportation infrastructure. The means to discover new places to drill without drilling a host of wildcat wells at tremendous expense was introduced by seismography. Enhanced well drilling technology allowed for deeper discoveries. Welding enabled a variety of occupations to become much more efficient. Innovations also attracted a new generation of employees capable of utilizing new skills even as they were absorbing the already well-established norms of a pervasive oilfield culture.

University of Texas survey crew in Pecos County, 1932.
Courtesy of Portal to Texas History

6 · SLOWING DOWN: THE GREAT DEPRESSION AND WORLD WAR II YEARS (1930–1945)

BETWEEN 1923, when Santa Rita No. 1 was completed, and the start of the decade of the 1930s, the Permian Basin's social, cultural, and economic configuration totally changed, leaving a permanent mark on the land. The drilling of Santa Rita No. 1 initiated a one-hundred-year oil and gas industry expansion that eventually encompassed the entire Basin. That process created an enormous amount of wealth, which in turn attracted many more people, who established a half dozen or so new towns along with hundreds of oil-company camps. The newcomers, all associated with the oil and gas business in one way or another, created an urban, industrial population that replaced the region's sparse, rural, ranch-related society. By 1930, the new population was also being linked by a transportation infrastructure that seemed to promise a bright future. But the next two decades were much different.

Although the overwhelming numbers of newcomers changed the nature of the population, the ranching industry stabilized due to the influx of oil industry wealth. In a 1970 interview Elliot Cowden, a member of a prominent long-time Permian Basin ranching family, stated, "It saved many of them from gone broke. They were so heavy in debt that I doubt they would ever have gotten out." In the same interview, George Bentley Jr., a lifelong resident of Jeff Davis County whose father was a Buffalo Soldier, reinforced that view when he said, "It was their salvation. They never could have survived without it."

In addition to tremendous regional social and cultural change, the Permian Basin underwent economic growth that profoundly influenced the expansion of higher education for all of Texas. The existence of more than two million acres of public lands, generally termed University Lands, whose earnings were placed in the PUF for the support of UT and later TAMU, lies mostly within the oil-producing areas of the Basin. Oil changed everything.

The Texas Constitution of 1876 established a "University of the first class" with an "Agricultural and Mechanical department." The latter referred to what became TAMU, founded seven years earlier with its own governing body. Eventually TAMU separated entirely from UT. At the time of this separation, income from University Lands went solely to UT. The question at that point involved defining the "University," as enunciated by the 1876 Constitution. TAMU claimed that they were entitled to a fair share of University Lands income because they were originally a part of UT.

The squabble continued for years, and a temporary settlement by UT allowed a token payment from leasing rights on University Lands to go to TAMU. In 1926 the stakes became much higher when TAMU began a serious effort to obtain part of the new oil money flowing out of the Permian Basin. As fate would have it, UT had more income than they could spend, but they were prevented by law from using PUF funds to construct new buildings, which they desperately needed. So, the two universities joined forces and worked out a compromise for sharing the PUF income and getting the law changed so that the proceeds could be used for new construction. The agreement went into effect in 1931 and allowed TAMU a one-third share in PUF revenue and

UT a two-thirds share. That deal has remained in effect to the present.

Since its opening in 1883, UT had struggled with funding. The original campus of forty acres had been expanded in 1921 by land paid for by the state government plus a variety of private donations. By 1930 that process had created a campus of 350 acres, but the legislature refused to appropriate money for new buildings. By then, enrollment had grown from the original 221 to well over 5,000 students. They attended classes in a hodgepodge of structures anchored by the venerated Main Building, completed in 1899. In 1932, UT devised a general plan of campus development to be financed through the newly expanded revenue from the PUF. Between 1933 and 1945 almost all existing structures were razed, including the Main Building. Its demolition created an uproar among alumni that was finally resolved by using the name on the new structure that was built on the site of the original Main Building. That first major use of PUF revenue changed the face of UT forever.

Much like the situation at UT, TAMU also received a decided boost in its first years of sharing the wealth produced by the PUF. From TAMU's establishment in 1876 until 1929, the state government had appropriated slightly under $3,390,000 for buildings and equipment on the campus. From 1929 to 1937, during the height of the Great Depression, utilizing the newly acquired PUF funding, A&M spent slightly under $3,166,000 on capital improvements. It has been suggested by many that without the infusion of that funding, both UT and TAMU would have been severely crippled or possibly even destroyed during those difficult financial times. As it turned out, both survived relatively unscathed other than a drop in enrollment.

Unfortunately for the Permian Basin's oil and gas industry, at the beginning of the 1930s there was no continued expansion; instead, a series of setbacks lasted for most of the decade. The first shock was the stock market crash in October 1929, which marked the beginning of the Great Depression. The second blow was the East Texas oil boom that began in October 1930. The first caused a general economic slowdown for the nation, and the second created such overproduction that at one point oil was selling for as low as ten cents per barrel. Between 1930 and 1932, Permian Basin well completions fell from 647 to 199. Although that massive slowdown caused a significant exodus of the newfound population, beginning in 1934 there was a slow but steady recovery that lasted the rest of the decade.

As the situation in East Texas came under control and oil prices rose, the industry in West Texas gradually revived, and Permian Basin activity began trending farther northward, away from the original discoveries. New fields that were discovered almost yearly did not create the massive booms of earlier years but caused a steady increase in production. Among those new fields were North Cowden in 1930, Means in 1934, Goldsmith in 1935, Seminole in 1936, Wasson in 1937, and Dune in 1938. While all that was happening, existing fields such as Kermit and South Cowden continued to expand.

By the end of the 1930s the Permian Basin was back to its original growth pattern. But oil production there remained somewhat subdued generally because of the distance to markets and inadequate pipeline service, which had always been a problem in the Basin. To service the newly opened fields and assure a continuing market, several new pipelines were built from the region to the Gulf Coast in the late 1930s. At the end of the decade there were eleven refineries in operation, including the original Col-Tex facility at Colorado City and Cosden's large new plant at Big Spring. Thirteen natural gasoline plants, used to strip the liquids from natural gas, were in operation, and two carbon black production facilities were running at full blast.

Population growth rose along with the recovery. A good example is Andrews County, just to the north of Odessa. In 1930 Andrews County had a total population of 736, with 200 living in the town of Andrews. After several discoveries in the area during the mid-1930s, by 1940 the county's population rose to 2,000, and Andrews boasted 600 residents. The bulk of the county's increased population lived in the 38 oil company camps built there, following the pattern set earlier in the southern part of the Basin.

Several new towns were established in those ten years. Almost all of them were small, such as Penwell and Goldsmith, in Ector County, and Forsan, in Howard County south of Big Spring, and none equaled the astounding growth of the boom towns of the 1920s. The only one that came close was Denver City, on the southern edge of Yoakum County. Established in 1939 to serve the newly discovered Wasson Field, Denver City was noteworthy for a couple of reasons. First, it was the last of the stereotypical tent-and-shack oil boom towns, and second, it was the first to utilize the newly introduced "trailer houses" that were destined to have a profound impact on the future of oilfield living conditions.

Denver City had a slow start. In a 1978 interview, H. C. "Doc" Cotton described the town's beginning: "At first there were no houses, only a store and a service station." Gradually tents and shacks began to coalesce around the store, but housing was so scarce that workers commuted from as far away as Hobbs, New Mexico, 35 miles to the west and Seagraves, Texas, 15 miles to the east, over roads that were little more than sand beds. In a 1979 interview, Locusta Ives remembered "a large flare down at the end of Main Street where men slept in cardboard boxes during cold weather, forty or fifty men at a time." Fortunately for them, a lot of work was available. As one eyewitness described the employment situation:

> You could count as many as 125 rigs running from any one spot in the field. They was paying good wages and they was plenty of work and you could double any time you wanted to. Back then if you needed a roughneck you would go to the pool hall and find

Andrews, in Andrews County, about 1940.
Courtesy of Portal to Texas History

one. Once I just quit work and took a few days off and when I was ready to go back to work I went to the pool hall and I seen this guy I knew. He was a tool pusher over seven rigs. He said, "I can give you any rig you want and any tour you want." It was that easy to get a job.

As always, with great success came new problems to be resolved. But modern technology could provide some solutions, in this case.

In recorded interviews, many people mentioned the large number of house trailers recently introduced into the oilfields. As early as 1936, the Stephens Hiway Home Company of Kansas City began advertising fourteen-, fifteen-, sixteen-, and even eighteen-foot models that provided "real comfort at little cost for field workers." Toward the end of the decade, these movable residences had begun to become popular as living quarters for workers who were following oil strikes across the country. In addition to that innovation, major oil companies built at least eight company camps in a ring around Denver City, in keeping with their practices in earlier booms.

With the opening of the Permian Basin to oil and gas development in 1923, San Angelo, in Tom Green County, had instantly assumed the position of the primary administrative center and equipment supplier to Basin oilfields. That was due primarily to its direct access via the Orient Railway. But by 1930, as new oil and gas development moved northward, the center began to shift to Midland and Odessa. They became homes to regional oil company headquarters and the affiliated concentration of the contract labor work force.

During the 1930s, Midland and Odessa experienced significant growth, although they never suffered from the uncontrolled, chaotic boom-town conditions of the 1920s. In 1920 Midland, about halfway between Fort Worth and El Paso on the T&P Railway, was a regional financial center, serving the ranching community in the central part of the Permian Basin. At that time, it had a population of 1,790, which by 1930 tripled to 5,484, and it had more than thirty small, independent oil companies. Meanwhile, Odessa, just fifteen miles to the west along the T&P tracks, was a sleepy little cattle-shipping point of 750 souls when the first oil was discovered near there in 1925. With the opening of nearby Penn Field in 1929 and the Cowden Field in 1930, the population ballooned to 2,400. It quickly became the oilfield service and supply center for the entire region. Over time, the initial division of activity between the two towns continued. Present-day Midland is seen as the oilfield management and financial center, while Odessa is the labor center for the Permian Basin.

The deciding factor that gave Midland and Odessa dominance over the region was tied to transportation and location. Both were in the approximate center of the Permian Basin on the T&P Railway with a direct connection to Fort Worth and El Paso, and shipping was very convenient. From the beginning, the commissioners of Ector County understood the advantage of improved transportation and began an aggressive campaign of road building in every direction out of Odessa. Better roads combined with the introduction of more powerful trucks like the Diamond T and White brands greatly improved load capacity, travel distance, and general efficiency. Motor-driven grading and excavation vehicles increased speed and efficiency in dirt work. Those changes soon made Odessa the new center for transportation in the region. By the mid-1930s, the day of the colorful teamsters with their thousands of draft animals dominating the oil patch scene had become a thing of the past.

Technology also sounded the death knell of cable tool drilling in the Basin as improvements in rotary drilling such as the tri-cone rotary bit, changes in mud technology, and numerous other improvements made well depths in the 8,000- to 10,000-foot range common. With the changeover to rotaries, the storied driller and tool dresser

Petroleum Building, Midland, 1934.
Courtesy of Portal to Texas History

image of cable tool drilling crews disappeared, to be replaced with the stereotype of the "roughneck" as the typical oilfield hand. Safety equipment was another innovation. Major oil companies like Gulf and Humble established and enforced formal safety programs, requiring such things as guards around chain drives and making roughnecks wear hard hats. New federal regulations mandated overtime pay for working more than forty hours per week, and the traditional twelve-hour tour was changed to three eight-hour tours per day (daylights, evenings, and graveyards).

Another innovation, developed in the Wasson Field, had to do with the completion of oil wells. As early as 1934, experiments in the Breckenridge area focused on injecting hydrochloric acid into newly completed wells in lieu of shooting them with nitroglycerin. In limestone and dolomite formations, the acid would penetrate spaces in the stone and dissolve it with the same effect as shooting without all the fracturing. Beginning in 1937, practically all wells in the Wasson Field were acidized rather than shot. The flamboyant Harrell Edmond "Eddie" Chiles, a pioneer in the acidizing business with his Western Company, declared that in 1939 he was treating most of the wells completed in the Wasson Field. He explained that the process was less costly than fracturing with nitroglycerin shots, and it left the wells relatively undamaged for later maintenance work. This innovation marked the beginning of the decline of the well shooter, whose expertise was no longer needed.

By 1940, things appeared to be almost back to normal in the Permian Basin with increased technological innovations, major transportation advances, and a growing demand for petroleum products. However, the looming war in Europe had begun to interrupt sales. The situation gradually became much more serious as the nation entered World War II at the end of 1941. That conflict put a hold on most of the progress in the Basin.

Despite its obvious importance to the war effort, the federal Petroleum Administration for War (PAW) put strict controls on the petroleum industry. One of the first things it did was freeze the price of oil and provide forecasts for the number of new wells necessary to maintain adequate petroleum products to fight the war. There was also a redirection of steel toward serving military needs and away from the petroleum industry, making those drilling goals difficult to maintain. As a result, between 1941, as the war began, and 1945, when it ended, there was not one new drilling rig built. Replacement parts were scarce, drilling pipe was almost impossible to obtain, pipe for new pipelines was hard to find, and new steel for storage tanks was out of the question. In the Permian Basin, that situation caused several small independent oil companies to suspend their operations for the duration of the war.

To further complicate matters, there was a decided shortage of labor to meet war effort needs. Oilfield work was declared an essential industry eligible for draft deferments, but many young, able-bodied oilfield workers opted to join the armed services as their patriotic duty and avoid the stigma of being called draft dodgers. Every employment level from roustabout to driller was desperately needed to keep up the production. As a result, the oil patch was forced to hire older workers and inexperienced younger people. To attract more employees, companies emphasized that the relatively new Fair Labors Standards Act, which guaranteed time and one-half pay for any hours worked over 40 in a work week, would be in effect. During the war years, most companies worked their employees 48 to 60 hours per week. It was also a time when many petroleum-related firms hired women to fill large numbers of jobs, usually office or laboratory positions vacated by men.

The front-line drilling operations were particularly hard hit by losing so many experienced drilling crew hands. J. D. Brown was an experienced roughneck who, in a 1960 interview, related an experience:

> I was working derricks out there at TXL [Oil Company] during the war and we was always short handed. Everybody out there worked all the doubles they could stand and a lot of the time we even drilled with a four man crew. Other than the drillers and three or four of us other hands they was mostly weevils (short for boll weevil) and nobody wanted to work derricks. Then one day the tool pusher come to me with a proposition. He allowed that if I stayed out on the job twenty-four hours a day all I would have to do was work derricks every time they needed to trip on one of his five rigs. The rest of the time I could sleep in the dog house and he would pay me for all the time I spent out there. Well sir I spent three weeks twenty-four hours a day sleeping in that damned dog house and living on baloney sandwiches. I thought I would never see another poor day.

With all that money to be made, a variety of inexperienced workers tried roughnecking. One of those was a big strong kid named Ralph Thompson, who was a high school student in Odessa. He got a letter of permission from his parents and took an unusual after-school job. He related, "They picked me up every day outside the school house. When we finished the tour, they would drop me off at my house after midnight. By the time school was over that year the driller even had me working derricks part of the time. I had more money that I ever had in my life."

Pipeliners and tank builders, on the other hand, did not have it so well. "Whitey" Harding, who had "broke in" building tanks at Best and Santa Rita in the early days, claimed that work was slow during the war years due to a lack of steel. He remembered that most of the work involved dismantling old tanks and rebuilding them using crews that were mostly boll weevils and winos. The same could be said of the pipelines in the Permian Basin in those days. There was no steel available to build those big pipelines.

Rig building, much like drilling, boomed during the war years. Every time a well was completed, the derrick had to be dismantled and rebuilt on a new location. In 1942, Gene Rumbaugh had considerable success with a system he developed for skidding rigs using track-mounted sets of dollies. A set of dollies would be placed beneath each of the derrick legs and the entire unit towed with a heavy dozer. It worked well in the level Basin terrain, and he even leveled sand hills to accomplish his goals. Of course, there was the occasional mishap, as W. R. Johnson recalled about a skidding job near Goldsmith. When one of the dollies dislodged, "That 120-foot derrick swayed left, then right, then toppled over. It was one heck of a mess."

Although most of the towns in the Permian Basin maintained a relatively stable population during the war years, the towns of Midland and Odessa grew from around 9,000 to 12,000 each as they consolidated their positions as the regional hubs of oil and gas activity. Once again, a boom situation created a housing crisis. This time the federal government created housing similar to that developed in California for thousands of aircraft and shipyard workers. Typical of the effort was a two-block residential housing development called Deep Pay Village in Andrews. It consisted of trailer houses, with their wheels removed, mounted on concrete slabs. Restricted to oilfield workers only, it was capable of housing two hundred families and filled up within days of its completion. In Odessa, there was a slightly different approach when one hundred prefabricated homes were built in a location called Victory Village. Both these facilities and others in the area were government-subsidized rental properties reserved for oilfield workers.

From 1930, at the beginning of the Great Depression, until the end of World War II in August 1945, Permian Basin oil production remained remarkably stable at 150 million to 200 million barrels per year. During the war years, the PAW estimated that the nation needed 75,000 new oil wells drilled, and despite the manpower shortage and rationing of needed equipment, the industry managed to exceed that by 10,000. By then, Texas had emerged as the largest supplier of oil and gas in the nation, with the Basin providing a significant portion of that production. But at the war's end the Basin's petroleum industry was in a shambles. Lack of adequate maintenance and replacement parts due to wartime shortages had severely hampered operations. The drilling aspect of the industry was particularly hard hit. Many oil-field people described the operable drilling rigs at that time as little more than piles of junk. On the bright side, however, was the fact that at the onset of the war there were numerous innovations in equipment on the drawing board that were destined to significantly rejuvenate the industry. That, combined with a returning work force, would create a booming economy in the immediate post-war years.

That little two-hundred-barrel-per-day producer dubbed Santa Rita No. 1 back in 1923 had sparked a process that proved to be unstoppable. It began with the remarkable oil boom of the 1920s that populated and transformed the social, cultural, and economic face of the Permian Basin as well as providing a solid endowment for support of the state's upper-level educational structure. The ongoing process survived the twin disasters of the Great Depression and World War II in more or less a holding pattern, with oil production holding around 150 to 200 million barrels per year and annual additions to PUF in the range of $1.5 million per year. It was time for the momentum to accelerate.

Oil rig in the Permian Basin in the 1950s.
Courtesy of Portal to Texas History

7   EXPANSION AND CHANGE (1945–1975)

THE 1920 UNITED STATES Census officially declared the country to be an urban nation with more people living in towns and cities than in rural areas. Texas, however, did not achieve that status until the end of World War II in 1945. In large part, the petroleum industry caused the state's shift from a rural to an urban society. Following the end of the war, Texas remained the country's leading producer of oil and gas, feeding a huge and constantly expanding petrochemical industry that stretched along the Gulf Coast from the Houston/Beaumont/Orange area in the far southeast to Corpus Christi in the Coastal Bend and on to Brownsville on the Mexican border. With a robust domestic market and oceangoing vessels available for worldwide distribution, the downstream Gulf Coast manufacturing part of the petroleum industry had an insatiable appetite for raw material. In 1945, the Permian Basin was on the cusp of providing a significant part of that raw material.

During the thirty years from 1945 until 1975, the Basin experienced steady growth in oil and gas production, significant population growth focused on the Midland/Odessa area, and profound technological changes in the nature of oilfield work and living conditions. In concert with that general economic expansion was the unprecedented growth of the PUF, which was fast becoming one of the nation's largest endowments in support of higher education.

The changes began shortly after the war's end, especially in drilling technology. Loosened controls on oil and gas production, combined with the end of wartime steel shortages, allowed the drilling industry to rebound quickly. One of the first innovations was the introduction of a unitized, portable drilling rig, dubbed a "jackknife" by the oilfield hands since its derrick could be raised and lowered like the blades of a jackknife. It soon replaced the old standard rig that had to be built and rebuilt each time it was used.

The new drilling rig could be assembled on the ground in several units. The substructure was set first, then the drilling floor was added, complete with draw works and engines. Then the derrick was laid down on the drilling floor, and the draw works, or winch, hoisted it into place for drilling. The entire process of dismantling, moving, and reinstalling relied on heavy-duty trucks and took only a few days instead of the two weeks or more it took for rig builders to dismantle and rebuild one of the old standard rigs. By about 1960, the legendary job of rig builder was another oilfield trade rendered obsolete by technology.

With equipment once again obtainable and manpower available due to returning veterans, drilling in the Permian Basin immediately accelerated after the war ended. Drilling operations rose 50 percent between 1947 and 1948 and again in 1949 and 1950. At the same time the number of small independent oil companies and major firms doing business in Midland increased from 135 to 356. By 1950, several new discoveries were made as deep drilling opened new pay zones in older oil fields. The net result was that by the end of the 1950s, the Permian Basin was producing the greatest amount of oil and gas of any region in the nation, with several new pipelines either in operation or being built to transport both products to market.

The first postwar boom of the magnitude of those of the 1920s occurred in late 1948 in the Canyon Reef Field, in Scurry County. Within a year, there were 187 rigs running in the field, requiring some 3,000 roughnecks to operate them plus a host of support workers to keep the operation supplied. It had all the indications of an old-time boom, including the associated tent- and-shack boom towns. But times had changed. The nearest town to the field was Snyder, which did indeed explode in population. Within a year it grew from a small town of 7,000 to an estimated size of 20,000. But the traditional "rag-town" look did not develop there for several reasons, all of which centered on improved transportation. Snyder could have grown by many thousands more, but many of the workers found lodging in Sweetwater or Colorado City and drove thirty to fifty miles to work and back each day. Others, permanently based in Odessa, which was approximately one hundred miles away, also drove back and forth every day. Paved roads and better automobiles made that possible.

The distance of travel to drill sites kept the Snyder's population from getting totally out of control. But perhaps the most visible changes in the nature of the boom town were the extensive use of trailers for living quarters and the almost total absence of shacks and tents. Samuel D. Myers commented on this phenomenon in one of his publications on the history of the Permian Basin:

> The most important living quarters were trailers, which by now had come into general use. It is estimated that 3,200 trailers were stationed on the streets, on vacant lots, and in parks provided for them, during the most active months in the oilfield nearby. The mobile home units are generally credited with preventing a housing crisis of serious dimension.

Mobile homes had come to define the oil patch landscape, replacing the cruder housing of earlier boom towns.

Just as the Snyder boom began to fade in early 1951, another one developed that summer. The boom in the Spraberry Field, which extended across seven Permian Basin counties from Borden County on the north down to near the original Big Lake find of the early 1920s, lasted well into 1954. The most active portion of that huge geological area was located thirty or forty miles southeast of Midland. Because of its size and isolated location, work in the Spraberry Field never produced a particular boom town. At that time and continuing well into the future, most of the workers lived in Odessa. A drive to work of one hundred miles or less was considered the norm.

At the end of World War II, drilling contractors generally paid their roughnecks only for the time spent on the rigs. But with the change in distance to the drill sites, they began to pay "driving time" at minimum-wage rates, with forty-five miles being considered one hour. The crews drove their own cars and the companies paid no mileage allowance. To defray travel expenses, a five-man drilling crew normally took turns driving, which meant that each roughneck had to drive only once every five days. There were variations on that theme, like the one related by Pete Sitton, who remembered that when he was a driller, he drove all the time and charged the crew fifty cents per day. Bob Cullen remembered those days as being hard on their work cars:

> Tires would only hold up for about 10,000 miles or so. They would generally hold up maybe six or eight months before they were ruined. We took pretty good care of our cars, but usually you could count on having to get a new one about every two years. Those old lease roads were so rough. Sometimes I ruined a tire the day I bought it.

Clearly, no one got rich from the money they got for driving their own cars to work.

Many of the crews that had been working for drilling contractors simply transferred to the developing boom area, but most arrived from afar, looking for work. The traditional hiring practice was to use gathering places like pool halls or cafés as recruiting centers. All those establishments had chalkboards, where job openings were posted. Jerry Holt remembered being in an Odessa pool hall late one evening when a driller jumped up on a pool table and announced in a loud voice, "I need a derrick man to work graveyards and I need him right now." He had one before he could get down off the table.

In Odessa in those days, there were cafés that acted as clearing houses for specific kinds of workers. For example, Dude's, on East Second Street, and later the Blue Top, on West Second, headquartered for drilling crews. Janey's, also on East Second, was home to tank builders, while Cookie's, on West Second, served roustabouts, and the Carol Café, on North Grant, attracted rig builders. The way the system worked was that the café owner put newly arrived workers in touch with potential employers. The café would provide the worker with a meal ticket, and the newly arrived hand's paycheck would be delivered to the café, which acted as a banker by cashing the check and deducting the price of the meal ticket. For an experienced oilfield worker newly arrived in town, that method supplied a useful service and at the same time assured the café of doing a thriving business while relieving oilfield contractors of the burden of constantly searching for help.

That long-distance labor pattern, a direct result of improved transportation, was also reflected in the growing population distribution across the Permian Basin in the 1950s. Except for the Snyder boom, general population growth in towns across the Basin in the 1950s was in a sort of holding pattern. Only three areas showed significant growth. One was Andrews County, where the population more than doubled, from 5,002 in 1950 to 13,000 by the end of the decade. The other two areas were Midland and Odessa. During the 1950s, those two towns, only fifteen miles apart, clearly emerged as the primary urban center of the Basin. As the Spraberry boom tapered off in mid-decade, Midland reached a population of 35,000, and Odessa topped 45,000. By the end of the decade, Midland stood at 62,000 and Odessa at 80,000. The reputations of those burgeoning cities remained the same as when they first began their relationship with the oil and gas industry during the 1930s. Midland remained the regional headquarters for oil company administrative activities, and Odessa was the operational base for labor across the entire Basin. That perceived difference between "company" people and "working" people created an intense rivalry expressed in every aspect of their relationship, especially in the sports arena.

Postwar growth created a severe housing shortage in both Midland and Odessa that was somewhat relieved by a massive home-building boom in both cities. But, just as at Snyder, the overflowing labor force turned to mobile homes for living quarters. During World War II, the mobile home industry had expanded as the need for wartime industrial labor skyrocketed. The average trailer was 8 feet wide by 20 feet long. By the war's end, manufacturers even produced 30-foot-long units. By 1947, six million Americans were housed in trailers. The size of these units restricted greater use, but in 1954 a federal law allowed 10-foot-wide trailers to be transported on national highways. At that point, portable family homes became a favorite residence for a host of oilfield workers, who had to move often as booms developed in far flung places. A survey of housing in Odessa between 1946 and 1960 illustrates that impact on the city. In 1946 there were only two trailer parks in Odessa. Within two years that number rose to 34 and by 1960 to 60. By then, the city of 80,000 had an estimated 10,000 residents living in mobile homes.

Also during the decade of the 1950s, El Paso Products Company established the largest inland petrochemical complex in the nation on a one-thousand-acre site just south of Odessa. It used natural gas from their wells in the Permian Basin. Between 1956 and 1958, butadiene and styrene plants were built to supply products for the manufacture of synthetic rubber at an adjacent plant built by General Tire & Rubber Company. Those facilities, acting as the anchor for the complex, attracted a variety of additions over the next few years, including an ethylene plant, a polyethylene plant, an ammonia plant, and other similar facilities operated by a diverse number of companies.

The vastly increased efficiency of transportation in the Permian Basin also created another major change in the region's traditional oilfield population distribution patterns. During the era of the 1920s and on into the early 1930s, lack of adequate transport made it necessary for temporary towns to be built close to the area of new discoveries, hence the establishment of those legendary boom towns. In the post-World War II era, the absence of those types of towns was directly due to an improved transportation system. By the same token, the huge complex of oil company camps that had appeared close to work sites became unnecessary. By the mid-1950s, those began to be dismantled, and by the early 1960s they were only a memory.

Technology also caused the demise of several other traditional employment skills during that same period. As noted earlier, rig builders became obsolete as the jackknife drilling rigs took over. Tank building also suffered a slow demise as welded tanks and, later, fiberglass vessels built in construction facilities replaced bolted tanks assembled in the field. Nitro shooters were gone by the early 1960s as high-pressure fracking and acidization took over well completions. A variety of roustabout work, such as laying temporary short pipelines, was replaced by extensive use of flexible polyethylene pipe, or polypipe, which was transported on a spool and rolled out as needed at a site. Although changing technology caused a host of other types of work to be no longer necessary, the one area of oilfield labor that grew significantly during this period was that of trucking. Somebody had to transport all that material to where it was to be used, and over time

Odessa became home to a massive trucking industry.

In the thirty years following the end of World War II, oil production in the Permian Basin experienced constant growth. During the 1930s and 1940s, production had remained generally constant in the range of 100 million to 200 million barrels per year, but with the end of the war change came rapidly as men and material became available and new finds came to light. By 1955 output had reached 500 million, ten years later it topped 600 million, and in 1975 Basin oil production peaked at an all-time high in the range of 750 million barrels per year. The price of oil, which had been frozen all during the war at less than a dollar a barrel, soon rose to the $4 dollar range in the 1950s and gradually increased over the next decade.

That thirty-year surge in oil and gas production, combined with the postwar increase in oil prices, was reflected by similar growth in the PUF. During the 1930s and the early years of World War II, PUF revenue was approximately $1 million per year; however, in 1943 the annual revenues began to increase, surpassing $8.6 million by 1950. Twenty years later, throughout the 1970s, it consistently ranged between $20 million and $30 million, averaging $30 million per year by 1975. That sound financial backing served both UT and TAMU well.

Enrollment at UT rose rapidly after the war. It stood at 11,000 just before the war, dropped to less than 9,000 during the war, and jumped to 15,000 within a year of the war's end. By the mid-1960s, there were more than 27,000 students attending school there. Over the course of the 1970s, that number exceeded 30,000. That massive increase in enrollment stimulated the construction or acquisition of 19 new campus buildings during the 1950s, many of a more or less temporary nature. Most of that additional space was underwritten by the PUF.

Further university growth was instituted in 1967 through legislative action that formally recognized the University of Texas System. As early as 1891, the Medical Branch at Galveston had been a part of

UT's operation. In 1919 the Texas School of Mines in El Paso became part of the system; it is now called UT at El Paso. Then in 1941 the M. D. Anderson Cancer Center at Houston came into the fold, and in 1949 the institution now known as UT Southwestern Medical Center was accepted by the Board of Regents. Next, Arlington State University, then operating as part of the TAMU System, was transferred to the UT System as UT at Arlington in 1965. In 1967 the Texas Legislature changed the names of all UT institutions to uniform designations and UT formally changed its name to The University of Texas at Austin to clarify its status as part of the system. During the remainder of the 1960s and 1970s, the system continued to expand, adding UT Dallas (1969), UT San Antonio (1969), UT Permian Basin (Odessa, 1969), UT Health Science Center at Houston (1972), UT Health Science Center at San Antonio (1972) and UT Tyler (1979). As those institutions entered the UT System, they also became part of the budgetary process of the PUF.

Just as UT experienced enormous growth and change in those thirty years, TAMU also enjoyed a similar pattern of expansion that was supported by the PUF. Just prior to the beginning of the war, TAMU had a fairly steady enrollment of around 6,500. It dropped during the war years to less than 2,000 but quickly jumped to the 8,500 range after the war ended. Nevertheless, over the next fifteen years the number gradually decreased to between 6,500 and 7,000 per year. Despite expanding its facilities and establishing research programs that enhanced its national reputation in various academic areas, TAMU was failing to attract a larger student population. University leaders finally faced the fact that the institution's slow growth was primarily due to its traditional status of having a military function, which required all students to be members of the Corps of Cadets and did not allow women to attend.

Throughout the decade of the 1950s there had been a determined effort by various groups to make TAMU coeducational and relax the mandatory enrollment of all students into the Corps of Cadets. But tradition is a difficult thing to change and struggles over the basic structure of TAMU often devolved into bitter confrontations. Ultimately, TAMU became coeducational in 1963, and two years later mandatory corps enrollment was dropped. In 1963 the university changed its name from the Agricultural and Mechanical College of Texas to Texas A&M University in recognition of its expanding academic reputation, while at the same time giving a nod to its traditional roots. Settling that dispute so expanded public access to Texas A&M that by the academic year of 1966 enrollment was well over 10,000, and by 1975 it had topped 25,000.

Back in 1948 the Texas Legislature had given TAMU formal approval to establish a Texas A&M University System. As early as 1917 Tarleton State University had become part of TAMU's system. With the view that was going to be a growing factor in the university's future, the system was organized with TAMU as the flagship institution. That would allow more growth during the next couple of decades.

The three decades from 1945 to 1975 saw significant maturation in the fortunes of the Permian Basin and in the institutions supported by the PUF. Oil production moved away from the early days of a colorful boom-town existence. There were still booms, but the many hardships and lawlessness associated with them largely disappeared. Much of that had to do with the appearance of family-friendly housing in the form of the mobile home, which attracted a more family-oriented worker. Better transportation allowed for a more stable, more centrally located, and more available labor force. And technological advancements created the ability to find and produce more oil and gas, which in turn created a strong economic base for the region. It is interesting that despite all the change and growth, the region's basic social fabric remained oriented toward the language and habits of oilfield workers, even with the influx of a host of newcomers to the region.

Additionally, those 2.1 million acres of University Lands kept pouring significant funding into the PUF in support of higher education. Both UT and TAMU grew substantially in enrollment, in physical size, and in academic and research excellence, supported in large part by the PUF. Both institutions began to expand their influence across Texas in those years as they added other smaller institutions to their systems.

Oil pump jack in West Texas.
Courtesy of the Library of Congress

8 DETERIORATION AND REJUVENATION (1975–2023)

BY 1975 IT HAD BEEN a little more than fifty years since the drilling of Santa Rita No. 1. Over those years, the extent of the Permian Basin had been more clearly defined as containing more than 25 percent of the land mass of the state of Texas, yet the inhospitable landscape supported less than 5 percent of the state's population. That population was overwhelmingly involved in the petroleum industry, which had developed a distinct regional oilfield culture. The Basin contained several thousand separate oilfields, most of which were discovered between 1923 and the 1960s. By any measure, in 1975 the Basin would be considered a mature oil-producing region. Beyond its reputation of being the premier petroleum producing area in Texas, it held the unique position of providing major funding for higher education in the state via the income produced by the PUF.

After producing an all-time annual record of 750 million barrels of oil in 1975, the Permian Basin began a gradual reduction typical of aging oilfields. A variety of secondary and tertiary recovery programs were initiated in older fields to extract as much of the remaining production as possible, but despite all that effort, by the year 2000 oil production had fallen into the range of 300 million barrels per year, very similar to that of the early 1950s. Then technological innovation again came to the rescue, and as the decades of 2000-2020 progressed, all previous records were eclipsed. The Basin again became the epicenter of oil and gas production in the United States, and the PUF became one of the largest endowments devoted to supporting higher education in the nation. Additionally, both TAMU and UT, in addition to being beneficiaries of the PUF, experienced tremendous enrollment increases and significant expansion in their respective university systems.

The narrative of change began in the mid-1970s when the Permian Basin was thriving. At the same time, national oil reserves were in a declining mode, creating a growing dependence on foreign oil and implying that the supply and price of oil was coming under international control. In 1973 a Middle East conflict between Israel and its neighboring Muslim nations prompted the United States and the Netherlands to support Israel, and the oil-producing Muslim countries declared an embargo of Arabian oil to those two western nations. This allowed the Organization of Petroleum Exporting Countries (OPEC) to increase the price of Arabian oil from $5.40 per barrel to $17 per barrel. In 1978 another international crisis arose with the fall of the Shah of Iran's government and the elimination of Iranian oil from the market. By 1980, the price of a barrel of oil was in the mid-thirty-dollar range. OPEC clearly controlled the price and quantity of oil on the international market, upon which the United States was becoming more dependent.

In the Permian Basin the reaction to the situation was mixed. Initially, with the price of oil increasing, there was somewhat of a boom, resulting in an all-time production peak in 1975. That continued into the 1980s. But despite the rig count rising significantly, production began to creep downward. Investment in exploration became more and more risky. Then in March 1983, OPEC cut the price of oil from $34 to $29 per barrel, and in October the First National Bank of Midland, the largest independently owned bank in Texas, failed. That marked the beginning of the end of major activity in the Basin as the price of oil became extremely unstable, fluctuating from a low of $7 to as much as $35 per barrel. The rig count immediately fell by half, and by 1990 the number was only a quarter of those operating in 1980. Numerous small, oil-related businesses failed, and the oil-patch's economy was in turmoil. It was a time of perhaps the greatest setback the petroleum industry had seen.

By that point, extensive, sophisticated seismological mapping, combined with thousands of drilling logs and core samples, had developed a comprehensive geological picture of the Permian Basin. It was generally well known where new discoveries were likely to be located. Innovations in drilling technology had improved the speed and efficiency of well completion, but there were no openings of significant new oilfields in the Basin between the mid-1970s and the beginning of the twenty-first century. All the tools were there to drill new wells, but the trick was how to find likely spots.

In the course of the Permian Basin's development, all wells were completed in sandstone or limestone formations, using traditional vertical drilling technology. That process advanced significantly in the ability to drill deeper and discover new prospects and use improved fracking and acidization techniques for more efficient well completion. Over the years, numerous fine-grained shale formations had been found to contain significant amounts of hydrocarbons. But all attempts to produce oil from them yielded little in the way of economic value. Existing vertical drilling technology and completion techniques did not work in fine-grained shale with its poor porosity. Many in the industry were aware of the problem, but there was no viable way to extract oil from those formations in paying amounts.

During the 1970s, George P. Mitchell, the majority owner of Mitchell Energy and Development Corporation, managed to weather the industry downturn in good condition and was successfully involved in activities in Wise County north of Fort Worth. He had encountered what he considered a major problem formation called the Barnett Shale. It was typical of marginally producing shale formations, but Mitchell was determined to develop a way to profitably produce from it. In 1981, he began experimenting using techniques that involved directional drilling and high-pressure fracking. Directional drilling was enabled by a down-hole motor connected to the drill pipe equipped with a rotating bit. The bit was powered by so-called "mud pumps" which pumped drilling fluid (mud) from the surface that allowed the bit and the drill hole to be steered horizontally through the shale formation. The process used sophisticated technology to control precise directional drilling, which facilitated long horizontal penetration. Over a period of sixteen years Mitchell spent an estimated $250 million and untold hours refining the technique, which used directional drilling and high-pressure "fracking" to release oil from those tight formations. He finally succeeded with the Barnett Shale boom in North Texas, which was soon followed by a boom in the Eagle Ford Shale in South Texas. The Bakken Field in North Dakota soon followed, and a revolution in the industry began.

The idea behind the process was to abandon the method of drilling the short distance vertically through the formation but to drill horizontally within the formation to access more of the reservoir. The horizontal portion of the well runs two miles or so and is normally fracked about forty times along its length. Then sand is pressure-forced into the fractures to keep the cracks open and increase porosity. Instead of drilling wells at some distance from one another, as was done in the vertical process, surface holes can be drilled as close as twenty feet from each other, with the subsurface well bores, which can be installed with 90 degree turns, diverging as much as five hundred feet to keep fracture fluids from leaking into another well bore, Thus, from one location several wells can be operated in close proximity and serve a considerable acreage.

The Permian Basin had several likely spots made to order for the new process. The first success came from several wells drilled in 2005 in the Spraberry Field, southeast of Midland, with considerable discoveries that reversed years of declining Basin production. Within two or three years, the focus turned to the deeper Delaware Basin of far West Texas, where long ago in 1921 in Loving County some of the first shallow Permian Basin wells had been drilled. There, both the thick Wolfcamp and Bone Springs formations produced tremendous amounts of oil. Two wells in 2018 each had initial flows of between 11,000 and 12,000 barrels per day. With the break-even price of oil at $40 per barrel and the market price fluctuating between $50 and $100 per barrel, the boom was on. The resulting activity produced more than one billion barrels of oil from the Permian Basin's western subregion in 2010, and this doubled to two billion barrels by 2020. The boom remained in full swing in 2023 on the one hundredth anniversary of the drilling of Santa Rita No. 1 and was greater than any that had preceded it.

The resulting flood of workers into the Delaware Basin subregion faced almost the same problems in the twenty-first century as their predecessors had one hundred years earlier when the Permian Basin was first opened to oil production. The activity was taking place in a sparsely populated, extremely arid area that was difficult to supply and maintain. The only difference lay in the massive changes brought about by decades of technological progress. Drilling sites in the Delaware Basin looked like used mobile-home lots, with a variety of trailers clustered around the rig, which was always the main focus of attention. The residences consisted of one for petroleum engineers, one for geologists, one for the drilling mud people, and others for a variety of workers actively involved in the process. The entire location was brightly lit after dark, like some sort of carnival, and could be spotted across the barren landscape from miles away.

The physical work of the drilling process remains pretty much the same, with roughnecks still doing the time-honored job of keeping the rig running. However, the process of controlling the drilling process has totally changed. The old-time driller, who in by-gone days stood by the draw works with his hand on the brake and his eye on the weight indicator to control the drilling process, was no more. The modern driller sits in an enclosed plexiglass cubical, with his hand on a control stick and his eye on a computer screen. His actions are supervised by a petroleum engineer in one of those adjacent trailers. The engineer tells the driller to adjust the direction of the drilling by two degrees left or one degree up or whatever is needed to keep the drill bit on target. Thus, the driller is no longer in total charge of his operation. Every morning, a report on the past twenty-four hours of operation is fed into a computer by the onsite petroleum engineer and wings its way through the ether to Dallas or Houston or Oklahoma City or wherever the company resides. There, the drilling superintendent can analyze the operation from afar in an air-conditioned office.

Despite the modern marvels of drilling and communicating by computer, there is still the unending question of how to house, feed, and care for the massive number of workers. During the history of the Permian Basin, housing progressed from shack-and-tent boom towns to company camps to mobile homes that could move with the booms without completely disrupting the social and economic structure of existing towns. A better transportation system allowed workers to live a significant distance from their jobs and commute. However, the new boom in the Delaware Basin presented a more intense version of problems that were historically familiar in the Permian Basin region. The location of the new activity was at the extreme edge of workers' ability to commute to drilling sites, and the arid nature of the area mitigated against establishing a new town or enlarging tiny Mentone and Orla, the only communities close to the action. A solution had to be devised. Man camps proved to be the best answer. A man camp is essentially a temporary dormitory-type facility composed of portable houses. It has sleeping quarters, laundry facilities, and kitchen facilities, all designed for living in a manner similar to motels, but smaller and more spartan. Workers live there for less than half what it costs to rent in town or stay in motels. In the post-2005 period, man camps appeared in or near the Delaware Basin subregion and elsewhere in the larger Permian Basin. They could shelter 200 to 500 residents, and at least one could handle more than 1,200.

The work of oilfield hands usually involves twelve-hour shifts seven days a week. They put in sixty to eighty hours per week, and they use the man camps as simply a place to eat and sleep. Normally, they have arrangements with their employers to spend two or three weeks on the job and then have a week off. That allows them, particularly those with families, to enjoy a relatively stable home life in places as distant as several hundred miles away without having to move constantly while enjoying good-paying jobs in the oilfield. At the same time, it provides oil companies with a reliable work force, and existing towns are relieved of excessive overcrowding and chaos, which are traditionally associated with an oil boom.

The long-term overall population growth in the Permian Basin remained relatively stable from the 1970s through the 1990s despite the slow deterioration of oil production. The resident population slowly migrated from smaller towns in the region toward the Midland/Odessa area. During those thirty years, the population of both towns grew from around 70,000 to about 90,000 each. Then, with the advent of the Delaware Basin boom, Odessa expanded to around 115,000 and Midland jumped to 132,000, according to the 2020 census.

The fluctuation of that fifty-year economic activity and its associated population growth in the Permian Basin was also reflected in the growth in the PUF. In the late 1950s, the fund was valued at approximately $250 million to $300 million. It then gradually increased despite reduced Basin activities, and by 1991 it was valued at $3.5 billion. During the mid-1990s the PUF increased its upward growth pattern, and in 1996 it reached the $12 billion mark. By mid-2022 it had grown to $42.9 billion and was expected to exceed $50 billion in 2023 on the centennial of the drilling of Santa Rita No. 1. As the PUF grew, the annual earnings distributions to the UT and TAMU systems increased from around $1.8 million in the 1950s to $1.2 billion in 2023, when UT had the largest endowment of any public institution of higher education in the United States.

During the same time span, UT at Austin enjoyed constant enrollment growth. Student numbers reached 52,384 by the time of the centennial of the drilling of Santa Rita No. 1 in 2023. In 2015, the UT system was reorganized with the creation of the Rio Grande Valley campus, which combined UT Brownsville and UT Pan American into a single entity at Edinburg. Then in 2023 the UT system absorbed Stephen F. Austin State University at Nacogdoches. Total enrollment in the UT system exceeded 256,000 in 2023, including more than 53,000 students enrolled at the Austin campus.

After becoming coeducational and dropping mandatory cadet membership in 1963, when it had an enrollment of 8,000, TAMU's enrollment increased rapidly to 25,000 in the mid-1970s and to 40,000 by 1990, culminating in 73,000 in 2023, when it had the highest enrollment of any college or university in the United States. In the late 1980s, it began a major expansion of its system with TAMU-Kingsville (1989), TAMU-Corpus Christi (1989), Texas A&M International University (Laredo, 1989), West Texas A&M University (Canyon, 1990), TAMU-Texarkana (1996), TAMU- Commerce (1996), TAMU-Central Texas (Killeen, 1999), and TAMU-San Antonio (2000). The total enrollment in the TAMU system in 2023 was 152,000.

The massive growth of both the UT and TAMU systems, with a combined total of about 408,000 students, had a tremendous effect upon higher education in the state of Texas. With the oil reserves of the PUF for support, both universities have significantly expanded their programming, along with enrollment. Ironically, this growth has overshadowed the continuing impact of the PUF, as the two systems have also attracted numerous research grants and a bevy of private donations to fund various projects. On the centennial of the drilling of Santa Rita No. 1, the PUF, which in the dark days of the Great Depression generated the universities' primary support, now accounts for only about 3.6 percent of the annual budgets for their respective systems.

Over the span of one hundred years, the Permian Basin's discovery, expansion, decline, and rejuvenation as a major oil and gas producer not only generated great wealth but had a major effect on the growth of higher education in Texas through the PUF. Starting as a small fund of little consequence that derived its income from grazing leases in a desolate, seemingly valueless region, the PUF became a unique support vehicle for higher education. Over time, its influence spread well beyond the two university systems to encompass the entire Lone Star State. And it all began with an impossible little oil well called Santa Rita No. 1.

Reunion of University of Texas administrators and Big Lake Oil Company executives at Santa Rita No. 1 in 1934.
Courtesy of Portal to Texas History

9 THE LEGACY OF SANTA RITA NO. 1 (2023)

MAY 28, 2023, MARKED the one-hundredth anniversary of the completion of Santa Rita No. 1. That oil well, which blew in as a relatively modest 200-barrel-per-day producer, derived its name from being blessed in the name of Santa Rita, the patron saint of impossible causes. The legacy left by that event could well be interpreted as overcoming numerous challenges to bring an impossible cause to a successful conclusion. The well's location, almost two hundred miles from the nearest known production, was developed amidst some of the most arid and forbidding terrain in Texas. Nevertheless, its success sparked a chain of events that opened up the Permian Basin to become the nation's largest oil and gas producing region. In the course of that, it changed a lightly populated and relatively isolated Texas region into a thriving, unique culture revolving around the petroleum industry. Additionally, as the first successful well drilled on the University Lands, with the income reserved for the PUF, it began a process that ultimately built one of the nation's largest endowments in support of higher education. From that inauspicious beginning has developed a tremendous legacy whose three basic elements of Permian Basin wealth, a unique oil and gas culture, and support of higher education in Texas are inexorably intertwined.

When Santa Rita No. 1 was drilled to completion in 1923, the Permian Basin had no impact on the state or national economy. There had been several preliminary geological studies indicating the likelihood of a large formation that might contain hydrocarbons, but its size and composition remained a mystery. Santa Rita No. 1 helped confirm the Basin's existence, and over time, as both oil and gas exploration expanded, it became apparent that the Basin extended some 250 miles from east to west and 300 miles from north to south, covered more than 75,000 square miles (48 million acres), and encompassed all or parts of 55 counties in West Texas and southeastern New Mexico. Further, it contained one of the world's thickest deposits of hydrocarbon-bearing sedimentary rock from the Permian geologic, hence the name "Permian Basin."

At first, drilling was confined to the 3,500- to 4,000-foot depth, using cable tool equipment and wooden derricks to reach what the old-time drillers called the "big lime." But it did not take long to discover that there were pay zones at deeper levels, beyond the capabilities of cable tool technology. Consequently, by the early 1930s the Permian Basin was dominated by rotary drilling equipment on steel derricks that drilled 6,000- to 12,000-foot wells. By the 1950s, exploratory wells were even being drilled to 20,000 feet. That technical evolution of drilling equipment, combined with the growing efficiency of geophysical exploration of the subsurface, created an ever-expanding growth in oil production.

Between 1923 and the early 1930s, oil discoveries expanded at a feverish pace, and the center of activity gradually moved northward toward the Midland/Odessa area. Then came a lull that lasted about fifteen years due to the combination of the economic downturn of the Great Depression and World War II. During that time, production from the Permian Basin grew from just a dribble in 1923 to more than 100 million barrels per year by the end of the war in 1945. After that, the Permian Basin experienced a thirty-year period of constant and often boom-like growth, which made it one of the major oil and gas producing regions in the nation. That culminated in 1975, when Basin production hit an all-time high of approximately 750 million barrels per year. During the next thirty years, although the Basin continued to be a major oil and gas producer, it experienced a slow decline consistent with aging oilfields. By 2005, production was similar to the 1950s, in the range of 200 million to 250 million barrels per year.

At that point, drilling technology made a breakthrough that allowed successful drilling in heretofore inaccessible shale formations. Beginning in 2005 and extending to 2023, that technology was applied within the Permian Basin first in the Midland Basin and later in the Delaware Basin subregions in far West Texas and southeast New Mexico. It provided a meteoric rise in production that topped one billion barrels in 2010 and reached two billion in 2020.

By the time of the centennial of the drilling of Santa Rita No. 1, the Permian Basin was home to 7,000 oil fields that had produced approximately 35 billion barrels of oil, as well as 120 trillion cubic feet of natural gas, in the century since the opening of the Basin. In 2022, the Basin produced an all-time high in hydrocarbon products that accounted for 40 percent of the oil and 15 percent of the gas extracted in the United States.

While the Permian Basin produced great wealth, it also spawned a unique oil and gas culture. During the one hundred years following the drilling of Santa Rita No. 1, the population of Texas grew by almost 700 percent, from 4.6 million in 1920 to 30 million in 2020. A similar surge occurred in the Basin, which grew from 270,000 in 1920 to 1.4 million in 2020, an increase of 418 percent. The constant element in the Basin's growth throughout those one hundred years is that, in spite of the fact that it represents approximately 27 percent of the state's land mass, it has remained lightly populated, consistently containing approximately 5 percent of Texas's population. Another difference in that growth is that the state as a whole has a variety of types of occupations, while the Permian Basin, focused on the oil and gas industry, has a unique regional culture.

Population numbers during any oil boom are notoriously inaccurate. Specific booms only lasted from one to five years, a time when hordes of young men, all temporary residents, rushed in to take advantage of the good wages. Most of the wild and wooly yarns concerning the colorful and lawless nature of the oil patch emanate from those short periods of frenzied activity, when wildly exaggerated estimates of boom town populations abounded. Mixed in with that crowd were many oil company employees working on a permanent basis. As the boom moved, a much-reduced drilling and production phase developed, from which an oilfield culture grew.

From the beginning, oil companies experienced difficulty in attracting solid, experienced family men to work in the expanding Permian Basin. Among the first efforts to solve that problem was the establishment of Texon as a company town designed to give employees a decent place to live away from the chaotic boom town environment. As oil and gas development grew across the Basin, attracting permanent employees continued to be a problem due to the chaotic nature of the boom towns combined with the arid and deserted nature of the region. That situation prompted the development of the oil camps that over time became a major element in populating the sparsely settled nature of the country with major oil company workers.

There is no precise count of the number of camps that existed in the Permian Basin, but they definitely ranged in the high hundreds. They ranged in size from as few as three or four homes to some that had hundreds of structures. The homes were built in a standard manner and usually had two bedrooms, with utilities and maintenance provided by the company at a low rental cost to the employee of less than

$10 per month. Streets and yards were also provided and maintained by the company. The larger camps often had swimming pools, tennis courts, and recreation halls for entertainment. They also had a significant number of storage yards and workshops designed to maintain the fields they served. They often sported dormitories, with dining facilities, used to house temporary workers brought in for special projects.

It is difficult to judge the influence of the camp system on the Permian Basin's population, but it was significant. Beyond living in close proximity within camps, bonding opportunities came from baseball leagues and other recreational activities. The camps provided no commercial facilities nor schools, so residents shopped and sent their children to school in nearby towns. Commercial and educational relations between the camps and towns created a situation which, in many cases, effectively doubled commercial activity in a particular community, more than the posted population of the town might indicate. Ultimately, that situation developed into a regional cultural norm with its basis firmly embedded in the oil and gas industry.

Although more permanent oil company employees lived together in a stable environment, contract workers represented the bulk of oilfield laborers. They were the roustabouts, pipeliners, tank builders, oil well service people, dirt workers, drilling crews, teamsters, and a host of others, and they were left to fend for themselves. These are the people who made up the population of the boom towns that grew up adjacent to any new significant discovery. Towns like McCamey, Iraan, Crane, Wink, Denver City, Goldsmith, Notrees, and Forsan are examples of those that survived, but there are scores of others that flourished for a short time before fading from the scene. During the 1950s, mobile homes began to be adopted by contract employees so they could take their families with them as work developed in an expanding oil and gas region. After that, large numbers of trailer parks came to identify oil boom towns instead of the ramshackle dwellings of an earlier era.

There is a definite evolutionary process surrounding oil boom towns. The first were overrun with mostly young, single men following oil booms across the country. They are the primary source of the towns' rough reputations. Living conditions were far from the best, basic living expenses were astronomical, and a general chaotic lawlessness prevailed. As soon as the oil activity began to subside, most of the first arrivals moved on to the next boom. The contractors who stayed to service a more sedate pace of oilfield operation, along with employees of the smaller oil companies, then became the core of those communities. Many experienced contract workers, as they married and started families, opted to leave the erratic pay of contracting for the more stable wage situation of the oil companies. In the late 1950s and early 1960s, when the camp system was disbanded, more company people moved into the nearest towns, further mixing the population and in some cases dramatically changing the size of some communities.

The oilfield culture that developed around this fluid, mobile society is a remarkably egalitarian one. After all, with a little luck anybody could become an oil baron! As Eddie Chiles once advertised, "If you don't have an oil well, get one!" If there is such a thing as a social divide among oilfield workers, it lies between the company people and the contract people. In the towns across the Permian Basin, there was a sharp division between company workers living in camps with normal amenities and the contract workers living in the towns where living conditions were akin to slums. In the post-World War II era, a proliferation of mobile homes filling the ubiquitous trailer parks in all the Basin towns tended to be identified with the contractors. Thus, a sort of social division developed, although both groups of workers performed essentially the same type of work.

That concept was carried further in the case of Midland and Odessa. From their first development as oil towns in the early 1930s, Midland had several major oil companies establish regional headquarters there, while contract workers tended to work out of Odessa. Midland became known as a company town and Odessa as a contract worker town. That reputation has persisted to the present and is manifested in many ways, especially on the football field, where a massive rivalry exists.

As in any industry, there is a certain language used peculiar to that type of work. The usage tends to overlap over from the workplace into general conversation. For example, there was the oilfield hand talking about a guy who stole his girlfriend. He said, "That boll weevil drilled right past me and set pipe before I even knew he was on location." Then there was the explanation by a roughneck about why he quit his job:

> It happened back in '55 when we were on a location down in the Spraberry. I was working derricks on graveyard tour on one of those Ideco Open View rigs for old [Homer E.] Whitey Starnes and I wasn't feeling all that good on account of twisting off down at the Hi-DE-Ho the evening before. Anyway, right after we got on location and it looked like everything was turning to the right Whitey decided we needed to come out of the hole and change bits. I wasn't about to round trip all those thribbles for the whole shift and I told him so. So we balled up our fists and got in a little squabble over it and he fell unconscious. So I took over and drilled the rest of the night until the tool pusher got there the next morning and fired me. Didn't have to handle thribbles of drill pipe all night though.

You can go into any café in the Permian Basin and hear that every conversation in the place is sprinkled with those types of words and phrases.

That lifestyle can be seen everywhere across the Permian Basin with roustabout trucks on the road, huge loads of drill pipe on their way to locations, oil tankers barreling down the highway, and highways crowded with a variety of similar transport. Early in the morning, convenience stores are crowded with men buying lunch material and filling water cans with ice and water. More often than not, the cans have six packs of beer at the bottom, to be enjoyed at the end of a long workday. The "washaterias" (laundromats) all have a section of washing machines reserved for "greasers" (oil-stained work clothes), and the cafés, pool halls, and other gathering places all have bulletin boards covered with notices of oilfield employment opportunities. Although the oilfield lifestyle is not confined just to the Basin, it is normally restricted to smaller areas or possibly to a couple of towns. Nowhere else does it cover such a large geographic area nor involve so many people. Indeed, what Santa Rita No. 1 started a hundred years ago has grown into a major cultural legacy that continues to thrive.

And then there is the PUF, created by the Texas Constitution of 1876 as the recipient of income from public lands set aside for the support of higher education in the state. Those properties, which by 1883 amounted to 2.1 million acres, were primarily located within what came to be called the Permian Basin. The 1876 Texas Constitution also established UT, which was designated as the recipient of PUF income. At the same time the Agricultural and Mechanical College of Texas was established as a branch of UT, although both institutions had separate administrations and for all practical purposes were independent of one another for decades before TAMU, as it became known, was officially designated as an independent entity.

TAMU held its first classes in the fall of 1876 in a rural area of Brazos County near Bryan on a campus the eventually covered approximately 5,200 acres. It was not until 1883 that UT held its first classes on a 40-acre campus in Austin that over time grew to a space in excess of 340 acres. From the first, there was a bitter fight between the two universities over rights to PUF funding. UT reserved the right to all the income, and TAMU felt they should get a share of it due to the fact that they were part of "the state University" when the PUF was created. Over time, TAMU gradually withdrew their complaints, due primarily to the small amount of income involved. By 1900, the PUF properties only had an annual revenue in the $40,000 range, derived primarily from grazing and hunting leases. When Santa Rita No. 1 was drilled on the University Lands in 1923 and oil royalties began to pour in, everything changed.

The first oil royalty payment to the PUF came in August 1923 in the amount of $516.63. By mid-1925 that sum had risen to $2,000 per day and continued to climb through the next decade. To say that TAMU increased efforts to lay claim to a substantial portion of that wealth would be an understatement. In 1930 things came to a head when both Texas institutions agreed to share the oil income. There was no argument that TAMU was a legal branch of UT, but the latter's Board of Regents was in charge of income distribution and did not want any of it going to TAMU. By law, funds from the PUF could not be used for construction, and UT badly needed to expand its campus facilities. Although there was a significant surplus in the PUF, none of it could be used to fund this expansion. Essentially, the two universities joined forces to get legal changes made to let TAMU share in the PUF and change the law so that PUF funds could be legally used to pay for buildings and equipment. The deal that was agreed on was that beginning in 1931 the annual income from the PUF would be divided, with two-thirds going to UT and one-third going to TAMU. It was a rare example of cooperation between those two competing institutions, but they worked together to improve higher education in Texas by sharing the PUF.

The results were immediately apparent when UT instituted a construction program that completely transformed its campus with 23 new buildings. It was the most substantial building expansion they had since opening in 1883. In a similar vein, TAMU inaugurated a building program. Since the college's founding in 1867 and until 1928, the legislature had appropriated $3.4 million for TAMU capital improvements, but between 1929 and 1937 the university spent $3.2 million on buildings and equipment. During the Great Depression of the 1930s, oil revenues from the PUF, in combination with revenues from the New Deal programs of the federal government, significantly enhanced the viability of both educational institutions. Many speculate they might not have survived without the PUF. As it was, both survived and increased in enrollment during those dark days.

The PUF and the two universities it supports grew significantly in the years following the end of World War II in 1945. Annual revenue ranged between $1 million and $2 million during the depression and war years, but the upturn in drilling activity during the 1950s rapidly increased that. By 1970, annual revenues reached the $20 million level. The revenues continued a rapid increase until they exploded in the early-2000s with the massive rejuvenation of Permian Basin oil and gas production. The market value of the PUF accordingly increased. During the 1950s, the PUF's value ranged between $200 million and $300 million. By 1990 it reached $3.5 billion, and six years later it stood at $5.6 billion. Then, with the massive increase in oil and gas production, its value stood at $33 billion in August 2023, three months after the centennial of the drilling of Santa Rita No. 1.

PUF's support of both UT and TAMU has been so vast that it is impossible to list all the efforts. But that activity evolved over time as the two universities have developed their respective systems to cover higher education all across the entire state of Texas. In the course of creating the systems, Texas Agricultural and Mechanical College changed its name to Texas A&M University and the University of Texas became The University of Texas at Austin in order to better reflect their position within their respective systems.

At the one-hundred-year anniversary of the drilling of Santa Rita

No. 1, both educational systems are huge. As noted earlier, in the case of TAMU there are a total of eight campuses in College Station, Kingsville, Corpus Christi, Laredo, Canyon, Texarkana, Commerce, Killeen, and San Antonio. The UT system now includes campuses in Austin, Galveston, El Paso, Arlington, Dallas, San Antonio, Odessa, Tyler, Edinburg, and Nacogdoches. All these schools, combined in two great systems, are supported in some measure by the PUF. In 2023, TAMU has an enrollment of 73,000 on its main campus, while the University of Texas at Austin has 53,082. The enrollment of both university systems is 152,000 for A&M and 256,000 for UT, reaching a combined total of 408,000, or approximately 50 percent of higher education enrollment in Texas.

There are many higher education endowments scattered across the United States, but almost all are dedicated to one university. By contrast, the influence of the PUF reaches across the entire state from Canyon in the Panhandle to the Rio Grande Valley and from Nacogdoches on the eastern edge of the state to El Paso on the far western perimeter. The legacy of Santa Rita No. 1 thus goes far beyond the opening of an oil field. True, that was the general result, but the impossible well had a much greater impact. The initial event, discovering oil, led to the development of the nation's primary source of oil and gas as well as providing a significant tax base in both Texas and New Mexico. As a result of that activity, Santa Rita No. 1 has been responsible for populating a major part of Texas with a culture that revolves around a single industry. And it has produced funds that support higher education across the entire state of Texas. Perhaps the development of the Permian Basin with such spectacular results was an impossible cause. If it was, then the blessing offered in the name of Santa Rita on that little oil well back in 1923 has brought good fortune to many and will do so far into the future.

INDEX

Unless indicated otherwise, all communities and counties are in Texas. Pictures are indicated by page numbers in italics.

A

Abilene, x, 3, 26, 61
African Americans, 43, 47
Alpine, 3, 27
Andrews, 53, 74, 81
Andrews County, 72, 73, 74, 89
Arlington, 93, 117
Arno, 5
Artesia (NM), 32
Austin, 21, 117

B

Barnett Shale, 100
Batson, 2
Beaumont (see also Spindletop), vii, 85
Benedum, Michael L., 21, 28
Bentley, George Jr., 70
Best, 14, 16, 18, 24, 25, 34, 40, 41
Big Lake, viii, 3, 12–14, 18, 20, 25, 26, 39–41, 88, *106*
Big Lake Oil Company, 21, 40, 41
Big Lake Oil Company Oilers (Texon Oilers), 43
Big Spring, 15, 72, 73
Borden County, 88
Borger, 31
Brazos County, 114
Breckenridge, 78
Brewster County, 62
Brookfield, 31
Brown, J. D., 79, 80
Brownsville, 85
Bryan, 114
Burkburnett, 2, 14

C

California, 81
Canyon, 104, 117
Central Basin Platform, 3
Cheyenne, 31, 34
Chiles, Harrell Edmond "Eddie," 78, 112
Cisco, 16
College Station, 117
Colorado City, 4, 72, 87
Col-Tex Refinery, 4, 72
Commerce, 104, 117
Corpus Christi, 85, 104, 117
Corsicana, 58
Cosden Refinery, 72
Cotton, H. C. "Doc," 73
Cowden, Elliot, 69, 70
Crane, 27, 31, 49, 50, 53, 63, 111
Crane County, 27, 28, 29, 51, *66*
Crockett County, 13
Cromwell, Carl G., x, xiii, 16, *17*, 18–21, 59
Cromwell, Carlene, 16, *17*
Cromwell, Luella, 16, *17*, 20
Cullen, Bob, 88

119

D

Dallas, 93, 102, 117
Delaware Basin, 3, 101–103, 109
Denver City, 73, 75, 111
Desdemona, 2
Doran, Paul, 40

E

Eagle Ford Shale, 100
Eastland, 2
Ector County, 46, 56, 73
Eddy County (NM), 32
Edinburg, 104, 117
El Paso, xiii, 3, 5, 13, 14, 20, 31, 61 75, 76, 93, 117
El Paso Products Company, 90
Erath County, 41
Eunice (NM), 32

F

Forsan, 73, 111
Fort Worth, 3, 13, 19, 27, 75, 76, 100
Fort Stockton, 3, 25, 40

G

Galveston, vii, viii, 92, 117
General Tire & Rubber Company, 91
Goldsmith, 46, 73, 81, 111
Grabble, Joseph, 44
Great Depression, 36, 63, 71, 72, 81, 82, 105, 108, 116
Gulf Oil Company, 49, 51, 53, 63, 78

H

Harding, Whitey, 80
Hertzog, Carl, xii
Hedberg, H. A., 40
Hobbs (NM), 26, 32, 34, 35, 58, 73
Holt, Jerry, 89
Houston, 85, 93, 102
Howard County, 73
Humble Oil & Refining Company, 49, 78

I

Iraan, 28, 30, 31, 34, 50, 111
Iran, 98
Irion County, 13
Ives, Locusta, 73

J

Jal (NM), 32
Jeff Davis County, 70
Johnson, J. P., 27
Johnson, W. R., 81

K

Kansas City (MO), 75
Kansas City, Mexico, and Orient Railway (Orient), 3, 14, 25, 27, 39, 41, 75
Kermit, 31
Killeen, 104, 117
Kingsville, 104, 117
Krupp, Haymon, xiii, 13, 14, 21

L

Laredo, 104, 117
Lea, Tom, xii
Lea County (NM), 32, 34
Lockhart, H. L., 4
Locklin, Dee, 18, 19, 21
Locklin, Nora, 19
Loving County, 4, 5, 18, 101
Lubbock, 2
Lufkin, 63

M

Magnolia Petroleum Company, 49
Marathon Oil Company, 43, 44
Marcus, Stanley, xii
McCamey, 27, 28, 31, 34, 35, 45, 64, 111
McCamey, George B., 27, 45
McDonald, R. S., 15
McElroy Camp, 49
Mentone, 5, 103
Middle East War (1973), 98
Midland, x, 3, 26, 53, 75, 76, 81, 85, 86, 88–90, 101, 103, 108, 113
    First National Bank, 98
    Petroleum Building, 77
Midland Basin, 3, 109
Midwest Oil Company, 32
Mitchell, George P., 99
Mitchell Energy and Development Corporation, 99
Mitchell County, 3, 4, 34
Monahans, 32, 64
Morely, Harold T., 26
Murphy, William R., Jr., xii
Myers, Samuel D., 87

N

Nacogdoches, 104, 117
Natural Gas, 72, 90, 109
New Mexico, 26, 32, 34, 35, 58, 73, 108, 109, 117
New York (NY), 13, 14
North Dakota, 100
Notrees, 111

O

Odessa, x, 3, 52, 72, 75, 76, 80, 81, 85, 87–90, 92, 93, 103, 108, 113, 117
Oil Fields,
    Big Lake Field, 21, 27, 28, 43, 59
    Canyon Reef Field, 87
    Cowden Field, 76
    Dune Field, 72
    Goldsmith Field, 72
    Hendrick Field, 31, 32, 33, 35
    Kermit Field, 72
    Means Field, 72
    North Cowden Field, 72
    Penn Field, 76
    Seminole Field, 72
    South Cowden Field, 72
    Spraberry Field, 88, 89, 101, 113
    Wasson Field, 72, 73, 78
    Westbrook Field, 4
    Wheat Field, 5, 18
    Yates Field, 28, 30, 31
Oil Industry,
    Employees, viii, xiv, 2, 6, 7, 18, 27, 35, 39–41, 43–45, 48, 60, 61, 63, 73, 75, 78–80, 86–89, 91, 101–103, 110–112
    Leases, 19, 20, 25, 27, 28

Technology, xi, xii, 57, 58, 67, 76, 78, 82, 85, 94, 98–101

Drilling, x, xi, 4, 28, 31, 34, 58–60, 76, 86, 99, 100

Nitroglycerin, 56, 64, 65, 66, 67, 78, 91

Oil Rigs, *iii*, 6, 8, 10, 14–16, 21, 59–61, 79, 81, 82, 84, 86, 91, 96, 108

Pipelines, 4, 5, 7, 31, 45, 63, 72, 79, 80, 86, 91

Refineries, 4, 5, 72

Tanks, 7, 20, 45, 64, 79, 80, 91

Oil Towns, viii, xiii, 39, 91, 11, 112

   Amenities, xiii, 27, 42, 44, 48–50, 73, 103, 111

   Camps, xiii, xiv, 19, 48–50, 52, 69, 73, 91, 102, 103, 110–112

   Culture, xiii, xiv, 5, 42, 44, 50, 52–54, 90, 94, 97, 110–114, 117

   Decline, 43, 44, 52, 53, 91

   House Trailers, 73, 75, 81, 87, 90, 94, 101, 102, 111, 112

   Housing, xiii, 7, 9, 15, 16, 19, 26, 39, 40, 41, 43–45, 47–49, 73, 81, 85, 87, 90, 94, 102, 103, 111

   Lawlessness, viii, 27, 28, 31, 39, 40, 44, 48, 94, 112

   Recreation, xiii,, 42, 43, 49, 50, 111

   Services, viii, xiii, 27, 39, 42, 44, 49–51, 73, 110, 111

Oil Wells (See also Santa Rita No. 1)

   Baker No. 1, 27

   Hendrick No. 1, 31

   Henderson, R. H., UT Well No. 2, 66

   Lucas No. 1 (Spindletop), vii, 1

   Rhodes No. 1, 32

   Russell No. 1, 5

   Skelly-Amerada University No. 1, 56

   T&P Abrams No. 1, 3, 4

Oklahoma City, 102

Orange, 85

Organization of Petroleum Exporting Countries (OPEC), 98

Orla, 103

Owen, Steven S., 3

P

Pecos, 3

Pecos County, 2, 28, *68*

Pecos River, viii, 2, 28

Pecos River Railroad, 5

Pennsylvania, xiii, 2, 16, 21, 58

Penwell, 73

Permanent University Fund (PUF), xi, xii, 11, 12, 22, 35, 36, 70, 71, 82, 86, 92–95, 97, 98, 104, 105, 114–117

Permian Basin, vii, 2, 9

   Economy, vii, ix, 53, 69, 70, 85, 94, 103

   Environment, vii–x, 2, 5, 97, 101, 102

   Oil and Gas Production, ix–xii, 1, 3–5, 11, 20, 21, 27, 28, 31, 34, 36, 59, 63, 69, 71, 72, 81, 82, 85, 86, 92, 94, 97–99, 101. 105, 108, 109, 116

   Population, viii–x, 3–5, 27, 28, 31, 32, 34, 35, 39, 40, 49, 50, 53, 69, 72, 73, 76, 81, 85, 87, 89–92, 94, 95, 97, 101, 103, 109

   Subregions, *xx*, 3, 101–103, 109

   Transportation, viii–x, 3, 6, 7, 25, 26, 31, 32, 45, 52, 61, 62, 63, 67, 69, 72, 73, 76, 78, 87–89, 91, 94, 102

Petrochemicals, 72, 90, 91

Petrolia, 2

Phillips Petroleum Company, 49
Pickrell, Frank T. x, xiii, 13-16, 21
Plymouth Oil Company, 43
Presidio, 3
Pyote, 32, 35, 40

R

Ramsey, Baden, 5
Ranger, 3
Rankin, 3, 27, 28
Reagan County, 12, 13, 24, 38
Red Barn, 28, 34
Ricker, Rupert P., 12, 13
Rio Grande Oil and Refining Company, 5, 20
Rumbaugh, Gene, 81
Russell Ranch, 5

S

San Angelo, x, 3, 14, 15, 25, 75
San Angelo Daily Standard, 20
San Antonio, 93, 104, 117
Santa Rita, viii, x
Santa Rita (1943), xii
Santa Rita (TX), 25, 34, 41
Santa Rita No. 1, *iii*, viii–xiii, 1, 3, 5, 10, 11, 12, 21, 34, 35, 39, 41, 53, 57, 69, 97, 106, 108, 117
    Blessing/Naming, viii, x, 16, 18, 117
    Centennial, 101, 104, 105, 107, 109, 114, 116
    Drilling, viii, x, 11, 14–16, 18, 19, 21, 59
    Lease, 11–14, 21
    Production, 19–22

Schwettman, Martin W., xii
Scurry County, 87
Seagraves, 73
Sitton, Pete, 88
Smith, Levi, 28, 41–43, 48
Snyder, 87, 88, 90
Sour Lake, 2
Starnes, Homer E. "Whitey," 113
Stephens Hiway Home Company, 75
Stiles, 20
Stillwagon, Crawford K., 16
Sweetwater, 87

T

Texarkana, 104, 117
Texas,
    Gulf Coast, xiii, 2, 48, 58, 72, 85
    Higher Education, x, xi, 1, 5, 11, 22, 35, 53, 70, 82, 86, 97, 105, 117
    Legislature, 12, 36, 71, 93, 94, 116
    Oil Production,
        East Texas, 36, 71, 72
        West Texas (see Permian Basin)
    Railroad Commission, 14
    Rangers, 31
Texas A&M University (TAMU), xi, 12, 36, 70, 71, 92–95, 104, 105, 114–116
    Campus, 71, 93, 95, 115, 116
    Enrollment, 71, 93–95, 98, 104, 105, 116, 117
    System, 12, 94, 95, 98, 104, 105, 116, 117
Texas & Pacific Railway (T&P), 3, 31, 32, 35, 75, 76
Texas Company (Texaco), 32

Texas State Historical Association, xii, 21

Texon, xiii, 34, 38, 40–44, 48, 50, 110

Texon Oil and Land Company, xiii, 13, 14, 16, 21, 41, 59

Thompson, Ralph, 80

Thurber, 41

Tom Green County, 75

Toyah-Bell Oil Company (Ramsey Oil Company), 5

Tucker, Hugh H., 15

Tulsa, 31

TXL Oil Company, 80

Tyler, 93, 117

Udden, Johan A., 12

United States, xii, 11, 85, 98, 117
   Petroleum Administration for War (PAW), 79, 81
   West, xvii

University Lands, xii, 1, 11–13, 22, 35, 36, 70, 95, 114, 115

University of Texas (UT), xi, 12, 68, 70, 71, 92, 93, 95, 104, 105, 106, 114–116
   Bureau of Economic Geology, 12, 34, 57
   Campus, 12, 21, 35, 36, 71, 92, 95, 114, 115
   Department of Petroleum Engineering, 36
   Endowment, 11, 12, 92, 104, 105, 114, 115
   Enrollment, 71, 92, 95, 98, 104, 105, 116, 117
   System, xii, 12, 92, 93, 95, 98, 104, 105, 116, 117

University Lands (office), xii

Underwriters Producing & Refining Company, 3

Upton County, 13, 27

Webb, Walter Prescott, xii

West Virginia, 2, 58

Westbrook, 3, 34

Westbrook, Roy A., 31

Western Company, 78

Wheat, J. J., 5

Wichita County, 14

Wink, 31, 32, 33, 34, 50, 111

Wink Townsite Company, 31

Winkler County, 31, 33

Wise County, 100

World War II, 78–82, 85, 86, 88, 90, 92, 108, 116

Yates, Ann, 28

Yates, Ira, 28

Yoakum County, 13